CAR TALK

A LEXICON OF AUTOMOBILE AND MOTORCYCLE SLANG

By the same author:

Hockey Talk (with Aaron Poteet, Robert Davies Publishing)
Plane Talk (with Martin Stone)

Cataloguing in publication data (Canada)

Poteet, Lewis J. and Poteet, Jim

Car talk : automobile and motorcycle slang

ISBN 1-55207-000-X

1. Automobiles - Slang - Dictionaries. 2. Motorcycles - Sland - Dictionaries. I. Poteet, Jim. II. Title.

TLP.P67 1997 629.222'03 C97-941056-8

Our ever-evolving catalogue is available on the World Wide Web at:
http: // www.rdppub.com

Lewis & Jim Poteet

A LEXICON OF AUTOMOBILE AND MOTORCYCLE SLANG

ROBERT DAVIES PUBLISHING
MONTREAL—TORONTO—PARIS

ISBN 1-55207-000-X

Robert Davies Multimedia Publishing Inc.
4999 Saint-Catherine Street West,
Westmount, Quebec, Canada H3Z 1T3

This book may be ordered in Canada from
General Distribution Services:

☎ 1-800-387-0141 / ☎ 1-800-387-0172
1-416-445-5967;

in the U.S.A. from General Distribution Services,
Suite 202, 85 River Rock Drive, Buffalo, N.Y. 14287
☎ 1-800-805-1082

or from the publisher, toll-free throughout North America:
☎ 1-800-481-2440 1-888-RDAVIES

e-mail: rdppub@vir.com

The publisher wishes to take this opportunity
to thank the Canada Council for the Arts,
the BPIDP program at Canadian Heritage
and the Ministère de la culture du Québec (SODEC)
for their generous assistance in its publishing programs.

Foreword

This book was really started before 1967, during the short life of our brother Steve, who died at age 23 in a motorcycle accident on his "beezer," west of Austin, Texas, in early June of that year. In the last year of his life, he wrote a paper for Roger Abrahams, his folklore professor at the University of Texas, on the curious fact that when Harley brought out the high handlebars, it tried to name them "angel wings," but the bikers themselves took over the power of naming and called them "ape-hangers," the name that stuck.

Co-author Jim Poteet finished his degree in English (with lots of courses in Classics) at UT, and then spent the next score and more of years fixing BMWs and Volvos, mostly, and occasionally any other car, from Studelacks to Toyolettes, in his college town. For a time he competed in enduro motorcycle racing across Texas, with brother Dewey, who won second in novice class, State of Texas, one season. Lewis finished his PhD in English at Minnesota, and in the 1970s began to publish little dictionaries of Nova Scotian and later hockey and Eastern Townships (Quebec) anglophone slang.

We come to this project from common experience, then, with words and with cars and motorcycles. Jim is fond of saying "my strongest faith is in the law of cause and effect." Lewis, who has been known to describe cars as "an unholy 'Rube Goldberg'-ish marriage of systems not ever intended by God to go together—fire and water, electrical-mechanical-hydraulic, rubber combustibles and solid steel—and all just to haul your ass down the road at an unlawful speed and at great danger to yourself and anyone near by," nevertheless is the proud holder of a Class 1 Quebec *permis de conduire*, a license to drive schoolbuses and 18-wheelers. We love motorcycles because they are minimal machines.

We've gathered these words about machines from Newfoundland to Mexican border body shops, with some British and European terms for comparison. Many were found in Texas, where they worship cars, but are in use widely throughout the United States. Most were heard in talk; only a few were taken from printed sources.

Like airplane slang (see *Plane Talk*, forthcoming from Poteet and Stone), car and motorcycle slang is rich in lively terms for how your machine can let you down, or things go terribly wrong on the highway of life. It can **go south** (or **west**) on you, **eat its lunch, turn turtle,** fail the **fry test,** develop **flat-spotting, throw a rod,** start to **knock,** be **FUBAR**, or **burn oil.**

You may be either one of the inevitable two victims of a **reverse gear hole-shot,** or suffer **gridlock,** or be **T-boned.**

These terms derive from a variety of sources, many of them auditory (you hear a noise, and it names the trouble—see **ping**), or sarcastic (see **go for throttle up, Challenger**). They may come from sports (**punt**), the military (**SNAFU**ed), the movies (**Buckaroo Banzai**), or the vividly visual experience of mechanics (**blue wrench**), racers (**chicharon**), and cops (**arrest-me-red**).

They express the mechanics' contempt for the ignorant, impatient, cheapskate owner (**id. tx., Sherwin-Williams overhaul**), the car salesman's contempt for the gullible buyer (**around-the-block guarantee**), the driver's contempt for the manufacturers (**mfrs, Fix or Repair Daily**), and also his suspicion of repair shop ripoffs (**carry a gun**). Above all, in words like **sushimobile** and **Kraut wagon**, they express everyone's fear of other cultures, when it comes to something so intimate as your vehicle, or, as the Hell's Angels put it, your **toy** ("the only difference in a man and a boy/ Is the taste of his whiskey, and his pride in his toy.")

The other side of contempt is pride. So there are words used like badges of honour: Ford, they say, also means **First on Race Day.** A gearbox you can **flog**, or shift hard and fast, putting it under strain, without breaking it, is **bulletproof.** Adroit, show-off driving is **cornering it on the doorhandles.** To race through a yellow light in Montréal is to **burn the yellow.** For real excitement, see **the hundred-mile-per-hour decision.** Or, if you're a teenager driving Daddy's car, and it doesn't have a **father-son switch,** do a **Lazy-J.** The lingo has words for the sounds of a lovely, powerful, smooth engine with a tuned exhaust, **winding out: coming on the pipe**, or the British **coming on song.**

Because the two authors of this book are on both sides, respectively, of the professional/amateur line, one a mechanic and one a non-mechanic driver, and because we inevitably notice what terms cross our path, our collection is rich in terms from the repair/parts shop and the customer/consumer, and perhaps weaker (though not totally lacking) in terms from the **mfrs.**

In the course of talking to everyone we could, everywhere we were, in the past five years, about cars and bikes, we have heard a number of good, true car and bike stories.

One of the best is contained in the entry under **cruise-control**, and it's too long to tell here. But, briefly, here are some of the others. Lewis, living in Montréal, has two that typify driving conditions in that lovely city bereft of smooth American freeways. One is about the underpass which kept developing potholes right under the bridge, which the workers kept repairing until they had built up the roadway to the point that the "clearance —- 3 metres" sign was no longer anywhere near accurate! The other records the fame or rather infamy of the Quebec driver who, at the entrance to the Ville-Marie expressway tunnel, pulled over suddenly, causing an 80-car pileup, because he didn't want to miss his favorite song, just coming on over the AM radio station. From Nova Scotia, there's the bittersweet tale of the depressed man who decided to have one last thrill before he ended it all, to do something he'd always wanted to do: he spotted twenty-two Royal Canadian Mounted Police cars parked in a row not far from the Halifax-Dartmouth bridge, and with his truck, he sideswiped them all, then raced for the bridge to drive or throw himself off it. Only thing is, they gave chase, caught him, and charged him with some hundreds of thousands of dollars damage to gov'mint equipment! Also from the Maritime playground of Eastern Canada, there's the time, in the summer of 1992, a fish-truck driver didn't see the sign, in the fog and rain, that warned of the end of the 103 semi-limited access highway and the T-junction, and in the resulting swerve and crash, left fish hanging in the trees and thirty gallons of diesel fuel in pools under the trees, ready to be set afire to cook the ultimate outdoor barbecue by the sea.

When we ask people for their favorite car stories, we've noticed that along with them, we always get stories that slide over into humor (often black humor) about other machines that inflate, deflate, or deflect human expectations. For example, there's Herman the Saw, the German train derailment specialist extortionist who demanded ransom, threatening to wreck a passenger train, and in an elaborate police plot to toss out suitcases of money and perhaps catch him, the plainclothes agent aboard the train was prevented by suspicious travellers from getting to the doors at the end of the railcar in time—they thought he was a would-be suicide—and by the time he kicked them out, they crashed into an oncoming train, scattering money by the gobs all over the embankment. Or the Digby lobster boat, overloaded at the stern as usual with pots on the first day of the season, which, when it met an unusually large Fundy-tide swell at harbour-mouth, pitch-poled and went down by the stern so fast that our informant said he saw crew members running up the deck and leaping off. (They were all rescued). Or again, the 250-pound practical joker power-boat owner who took friends for a fast, drunken ride on his jet-boat, and feigned a heart attack, falling forward onto the throttle and jamming his hammy arm through the steering wheel so they couldn't lift him off, just as they were headed directly for the side of an oil tanker. At the last minute . . .

What's interesting about the mix of these stories points directly to the central subject, if somewhat hidden, of this book. These words and phrases are ultimately about the human interface with technology, how machines make us feel good and powerful, how they test our control, and how our best, cleverest schemes and devices sometimes go awry, with consequences so devastating that ... what can we do but talk and laugh about it?

We see the automotive and motorcycle worlds as a major part of North American culture, strongly male and redneck as it is. And we offer this collection as a sort of index to that culture.

Some of the phrases in this book, when spoken, may be offensive to some listeners. In a world in which "monkey see, monkey do," we would not have it taken as a recommendation from us that we include a phrase. We are not responsible for the disgusting feelings held by some of our fellow speakers of English. One of us is not an English teacher (those widely regarded as setting norms for correct speaking), and the other, who is, here is working as a researcher. This is not a book about how to talk; it is a record of, and a book about, hearing, listening, and understanding.

A

A — the MGA, a British sportscar, "sleek but slightly bulbous," made between 1955 and 1962, after wing fenders and before the **B** (the MGB). Above all, the first mass-produced sports car, with generous use of cardboard for interior body paneling. The Triumph used cardboard (pasteboard, paperboard) for transmission tunnel device!

Abarth — Carlo Abarth, Italian carmaker, Turin. Now manufacturer of exhaust systems for Fiat and other aftermarket systems. "If you want your BMW to sound like a Fiat, put an Abarth exhaust system on it. "

A. B. S. — automatic braking system, German designed and shared by BMW, Porsche, Mercedes-Benz, etc. Idiot-proof computer senses wheel lockup point and automatically releases brake. Hard braking feels like a series of pulses, damned effective, even in rain and snow.

AC — "AC" Cobra. Small four-wheel independent suspensioned British sports car which Carroll Shelby made into a monster with Ford V-8 (in two versions, 289 and 427 cubic inches, respectively). The 427 was nicknamed the **Thunderlizard**, though the 289 often had faster lap times.

AC juice — Freon 12, used for automobile air conditioning systems, as distinguished from Freon 22, used in house air conditioning. "It needed 2 cans of AC juice, but it spits ice now." Freon is dichlorophoromethane.

advancing to the rear — "This means a driver is losing the race and falling back from the lead." From C. H. B. in the San Antonio *Current* the day before the San Antonio Gran Prix (1988).

aerial — British term for "antenna."

aeroscreen — small windshield (s) in front of driver (& passenger) in lieu of full width (U. K.).

aging gracefully — rural experts agree no vehicle ages more gracefully and slowly than the 1950s Chevy pickups, especially the green ones. "Hell, Homer, don't paint it," the body man is saying, "that green is so baked on by the sun it'll be there forever...and it ain't gonna rain anyhow....those little rust spots ain't getting any bigger....it's aging gracefully."

air bag — back seat driver, i. e. a person who criticizes the driver incessantly.

air dam — the rubber or fiberglass bumper extension hanging down from the front bumper on **muscle cars**, also known as a **spoiler.** (Technically, a spoiler is an aerodynamic aid attached to the top or upper rear of the vehicle, to resist the tendency to rise at high speeds, but common speech often ignores such technical distinctions).

- Don't usually help your car's lift coefficient until you reach 70mph plus.
- Don't help you get off with warning tickets.

Those speed bumps they put in the Safeway parking lot efficiently remove low hanging equipment such as air dams and spoilers.

airfoil — wing attached to race car which creates aerodynamic downforce, to hold car on track at high speeds.

Alfalfa — Alfa Romeo (as nicknamed at Dynatune Motors, Montreal, Quebec, during the 1970s). Also known as **Awful Romeo.**

ALFA ROMEO — **A**ssociation **L**ombardi **F**abricationi **A**utomobile **Romeo.**

Alfetta, Alphaguish — pet names by Italian Alfa owners (*Alfisti*) for their car.

Allanté — name of a 1980s model of Cadillac, a word that "means nothing in any known language, like Exxon and Häagen-Dazs," according to John McPhee in the Dec. 4 1989 *New Yorker.* The word does suggest "allons," French for "let's go!"

Allison V-12 — engine used on rail jobs in the top fuel dragster class, AA Unlimited, and also to power the P-51 Mustang fighter aircraft. (The P-51 was even more successfully powered by a Packard Merlin, from Rolls Royce Merlin built under license). In Formula I racing, the cars were lighter but still had enormous (3-6 litre capacity, up to 24 cylinder) engines.

AMC — officially American Motors Corporation, the parts guys at Dale's in Austin TX call them "Acme", partly because of the similarity of the initials, partly because of the "low bidder reputation" of AMC cars, which used some General Motors components (alternators, e. g.) and some Ford (carburetors). And partly because of Wile E. Coyote's supplier of practically all technical equipment in his cartoon battle against that well-known scofflaw, RoadRunner.

Americans — "spoke style mag wheels." —from Paul Burrill, Madison WI.

American stop — see **rolling stop.**

AMG — Mercedes Benz 500 SEL. The letters AMG stand for the first letter of the name of the town where the car is specially modified (Affaltenberg), and "Motoren Gesellschaft," by the Swabian (name of the region) Tuning Company.

amphi-car — Triumph with propellers, a slightly modified Triumph Herald. Sank rapidly when bumped or even slightly punctured by pointed underwater obstacles such as rocks.

Amphicar's debut in Austin was short and wet. Entering (driving into) Town Lake at Red Bud Isle (site of old dam which ruptured in 1920), the Amphicar representative, the exalted Mayor of Austin, and the owner of the "Pit Stop", soon to be exclusive dealer, felt the impact....The Amphicar had stopped. Engaging reverse, they backed off the rock...

"We're sinking," the mayor exclaimed. Indeed, water already around their ankles.....The Amphicar had struck a square chunk of granite, a piece of the old dam. With Channel 7 filming it, the Amphicar sank like an open safe, leaving the exalted three personages swimming frantically toward shore in their three-piece suits.

"How much do you want for that film you just took...." the Amphicar rep spluttered, water still streaming off him.... "How much," he insisted....."how much?"

anchors — see **binders.**

ancient Mesopotamian cooking techniques — "Have we got a radio show for you folks today," one of the brothers on National Public Radio's Car Talk is saying: "we have everything from Ancient Mesopotamian cooking techniques to carburetors."

We assume that these Northeasterners are referring to what is known down South as "old Spanish tricks," i. e. Ned, the apprentice mechanic asks, "How are you going to get that chingered nut off?"

"It's an ancient Mesopotamian cooking technique. You get something with fire coming off it (lights torch—"**smoke wrench**") aaaand, heat it like so (moves fire from torch round and round the nut), cooking it slowly.....See, old Spanish trick, ...smoke wrench."

Anderson cart — "An Anderson cart is, or rather was, a cart made from a cut-down car and pulled by horses. Named after Premier Anderson of Alberta, it originated during the depression, as did the **Bennett Buggy.** It should not, however, be confused with the latter, which is markedly different in appearance. Whereas the Bennett buggy was essentially a towed car, the Anderson cart was a cart made from a car chassis with much of the body, and in some cases the front two wheels, removed.

The naming of the two vehicles after politicians was neither a mark of respect nor an indication that they developed the vehicle. Rather, it reflected the blame placed on the politicians for the hard times of the depression." —Chris Thain, in *Cold as a Bay Street Banker's Heart: The Ultimate Prairie Phrase Book* Western Producer Prairie Books, Saskatoon, Sask., 1987.

antbed relay — Chrysler relays, *hecho in Mexico*, which have insulation substance that ants love to eat away, picnic in, etc. Renders the circuit inoperative.

antisubmarine strap — part of racing safety belt harness. Goes between the legs, to prevent driver from slipping (submarining) down through belt restraint system. So wear your cup.

ape-hangers — bikers' term for high handlebars, quickly invented after the option appeared, to replace the term Harley-Davidson tried to market them with, "angel wings." —from Steve Poteet.

apex — the point in a turn, in car racing, where the driver is closest to the inside, just before the car begins drifting back outside.

apron — inside edge of paved race track. You come off the track onto the apron, then into the pits.

arced plug —a spark plug whose electrical path has been shortened, i. e. the spark, instead of jumping across the proper electrode, goes through the insulator ceramic, causing a dead miss on that cylinder. Especially unfortunate if you have only one cylinder, as on small British bikes and German 50cc mopeds using 16:1 fuel/oil mix (2-strokes).

around the block guarantee — see **out of sight guarantee.**

arrest-me-red — a bright, eye-catching red, applied in many coats to a hot rod. A color that speaks...er....screams for itself. Eye-catching paint job on a hot rod show car (from TV show "Crazy about Wheels").

ASC — automobile stability control (auto skid control). German-built system, senses relative wheelspin (say, wheels in gravel), and yer foot (pedal to the floor?) and cuts engine power until wheelspin is under control. Idiot and teenager-proofing at its German finest. Available on European model cars only at this point.

ass-sembled — not assembled. Ace says this of American cars. "Body by Fisher," he snorts....."Used to be real good bodies....windows all roll up and down real easy and good......now...." He sniffs. "Every day is Monday or Friday in those plants."

asswipe gearshift — an early Harley had a gearshift behind the seat and below, which, to manipulate, required the driver to reach behind and down.

Austin Healey — now that they're gone, we can talk about them. Oil leaking, hard to work on, questionable handling, Lucas electrics (see **Prince of Darkness**), and a great sound from the pipes. Collectors' item sports car. Makers of the **Bug-eye Sprite.** The Austin-Healey 100, later called the 3000, models were strikingly clean in design, with very few motifs, an unusual elegant sports car. Healey Silverstone had a spare wheel mounted *as* rear bumper, on side, *set into* the trunk (or, properly speaking, **boot**).

auto alarms — some have sirens, some shut down the fuel system when the car is broken into. The nasty one is the one that doesn't sound the horn or activate the police alarm, but rather sounds a beeper on the owner's hip Sometimes known as the "G. Gordon Liddy/Rambo model," because the owner can come creeping up, silently on the intruder. (Colonel Willis, Austin TX, has one. He's been through it before and wants to deal with the intruder-thief himself.)

Necessary bane of life in Los Angeles luxury condo neighbourhoods. Alarms are always going off early in the morning and late at night, usually due to malfunction or the car being bumped accidentally.

The "James Brown alarm" goes "OOOW, OOOW, OOOW."

Autohenge — an outdoor visual sculpture garden near Oshawa, Ontario, where Bill Lishman has buried rusted hulks of car bodies at the same depth so they protrude as far as the monoliths at England's famed Stonehenge. There are *forty* crushed cars, and the uprights are American car bodies, the "lintels" or cross-pieces, Japanese. For photo, see Jan. 1989 *Car & Driver.*

automotive styling and design — (U. S.) There was a General Motors vice-president named Harley Earl "who held that cars that looked better than they worked would make buyers want them more than they needed them." —Malcolm Parry, "Dash to the Future," *En Route* (inflight magazine for Air Canada), November 1992.

Auto-Union — old name for Audi, now of course part of Volkswagen. Kings of motor racing around 1938.

Studebaker **Avanti** — now defunct car company's fastest car. 1962 model had supercharged V8 with 280 hp.

Awful Romeo — a nickname for the Alfa Romeo, applied at Montreal's Dynatune Motors during the 1970s.

B

B — affectionate term for a MGB, British sportscar.

baby buggy — old VW Beetle convertible, after the way the top folds down to make it look like a baby buggy.

baby Corvette — The Opel GT. Looks like a little Vette, doesn't accelerate like one.

baby moons — U. S. (especially Southwest) version of **moons.**

baby's got a new pair of shoes — a way of noticing that a car has a new set of tires. Also, a **new set of skins.**

backing — American term for "reversing." —British entry

back-marker — in racing, the lap bike or car. Hence, drivers going slower than you may be jocularly dubbed "back-markers," because you pass them a lot if you're placing high in the order. Front-runners can use them for strategic advantage—i. e. get around them before tight corners and leave your competition stuck behind them there.

back seat driver — the job nobody should want, as it is based on an absurd, prideful, ignorant notion that a person sitting anywhere but in the driver's seat can see everything that's happening and decide what moves the driver should make to ensure a good trip. Surprising, isn't it, that people get this idea—and not only wives, but fathers of driving daughters, etc. See **airbag.** However, even the best driver can always use a good lookout, **riding shotgun.**

bad boy car — the sort of car that gets no mercy from police. It is visibly a high-performance, modified, **souped up** vehicle. I. e. Hurst-Olds (Hurst drag-race shifter on Oldsmobile), red Corvettes—rear seat and bumpers removed from BMW, blacked-out grilles, aerodynamic packages (skirting), fat tires.

badge engineering — creating an entirely new car by putting a different badge on an existing car. Austin Healey Sprite Mk II and

MG Midget Mk I are examples; so are the Omni-Horizon products from Chrysler. See **Omnirizon.**

bad road — in "she has a face like twenty miles of bad road," car talk is adapted to bar discourse. College students apparently have it as "five miles", but the lines and the highways seem to come together in male talk about prostitutes....... See **hi mileage.**

Bahnburner — a really fast German car, BMW, Porsche, Mercedes-Benz, etc. A pun on "barnstormer" and "barnburner," deflecting the sounds off toward "autobahn," the German term for "freeway", which in Germany has no speed limit. On German radio, you may actually hear broadcast the in-car conversations of high-tech mechanics road-testing new fast cars at 220 kilometres per hour on the autobahn.

A "barnstormer" is an old slang term for a stunt pilot who in the early days of aviation would tour from town to town, from fair to fair, but especially from field to field (hence "barnstormer") doing daredevil flying.

"Barnburner," in turn, is a term for a particularly wild and dangerous species of poor white trash redneck human (the Snopeses in William Faulkner's fiction) who would take their revenge for real or imagined insults or oppression by threatening (or carrying out) the action implied in "Tell him [the plantation owner] wood an' hay kin burn......"

Bahn rules — left lane, fast lane....one must yield to faster car. Trucks keep to the right lane only. We oughta do it here.

balanced in blueprint — rhyming slang for engineers' procedure.

baling wire — legendary, rulebending fastener, like duct tape, necessary in emergencies. But not used by mechanics at the Mercedes dealership. They, it is said, use the *smaller gauge twist tie* wire, plastic coated so it won't rattle, found tying ends of loaves of bread.

balloon in the spokes engine — engine of childhood. Any kid who had a bicycle knew that if you inflated a balloon, then tied it to the frame of the bike, right next to where the spokes of the rear wheel went by, when you pedaled, the balloon became involved with the spokes, rubbing against each spoke in rapid succession as the bike went faster and faster. The device made a great sound, which got more and more satisfying and louder and louder the faster one went, until the balloon broke. Car engines are much the same..... A British car fanatic reports that he used folded cigarette packets.

balloon skirts — especially large, flashy **fender skirts,** which covered the area from the front of the rear wheel opening to the rear of the car, actually enclosing part of the fender.

balls to the wall — describes the driving skill and nerve of a courageous race car driver. A term from the car talk of, and here remembered in honor of Stephen Dallas Poteet, who died with his balls to the wall, June 7, 1967.

banana peels — bald, slick military surplus tires, sold after long use has worn them smooth.

bananas in the crankcase — extra heavy oil put into an engine to cover up **knocking,** caused by serious internal damage, so the car may be resold. —from Robert Appel's *The Used Car Believer's Handbook.* For the British variation on this dirty trick, see **sawdust in the differential.**

band aid —factory "fix" for problem originally caused by poor design (i. e. interruptor switches which cut off your air conditioning compressor, which draws lots of power, during hard accelerating, sharp turns, braking, etc., especially on 1600cc Ford Escort, Mercury Lynx, etc.)

banger — Brit. term for **beater, bazou, clunker.**

banjo — the rear end, from the shape of the differential and axles coming out from it.

Banzai runners — California bad boys observed but seldom caught. Devil-may-care Porsche/Ferrari etc. drivers going 130 mph, weaving in and out of traffic on the LA freeway. Inspired by Buckaroo Banzai in the 8th Dimension, movie.

Baptist bag — small brown paper bag used to conceal ("make legal" to consume in public, i. e. and in your car, in the good old days) a bottle, usually of beer. "You want a Baptist bag with that beer, buddy?" — Texas "roadway Circle K", 1959.

Barris — George Barris, master custom car builder of 1950s California. It was Barris who "styled" a Rolls-Royce for Zsa Zsa Gabor. Originally owned by the Duchess of Kent, Kustom Industries (i. e. Barris) gold-plated the mascot, finished the car in "thirty coats of Murano Pearl of Essene two-tone gold paint, [put] Zsa Zsa's signature on the radiator badge, and built in walnut wine and make-up cabinets." —Fox & Smith, *Rolls-Royce: The Complete Works.* The car was bought at a Hollywood car auction in 1983 by Henry Kurtz (Krazy Kar Museum, NJ), who also owns the original Batmobile ("for my son to drive").

barking the tires — not **burning off**, but making the tires produce a sharp sound by popping the clutch during a shift while moving. The trick it to have the motor **revving** at a different speed (faster or slower, it doesn't matter which) when the clutch is re-engaged than it was when it was released. However, Don Hackett has pointed out that when it is done by decelerating, you may be in danger of swapping ends.

barrel-back with barn doors — 1946 Ford Monarch, which had wood trim, doors & trunk.

barstool — a vehicle, especially a motorcycle or motorscooter, you own and keep around but never ride, because....it needs work, or really just never gets used. "I'm gonna sell the Lambretta and use the money to go to Belize. I love it, but it's just a barstool, really." The name comes from the habit of sitting on the vehicle and reminiscing about when you *used* to ride it, or one like it.....Lambrettas make good barstools because they're easy to turn over.

basket case — home mechanic's botched job, brought to the mechanic so it can be done right. The term, which in general parlance usually is applied to persons in mental distress, is sometimes literally true of a car repair job: the parts are carried into the shop in a *basket or box.* It is even more common in bike repair shops.

basket-handle — descriptive nickname for the feature of certain new GM convertibles which the Montreal Gazette auto supplement calls "roll-bar styled strip [which] loops over mid-section of car to produce extra rigidity required when roof is ripped off." (Jan. 11, 1990)

bastard — any car which has an important part, like the motor, from another car. The classic example is a Jaguar with a Chevy engine.

Bauhaus on wheels — a Volkswagen Beetle, according to Malcolm Parry in the November 1992 *En Route* magazine (in-flight publication for Air Canada). The name refers to the simplicity and functional character of the design of this popular compact car.

Bavaria — large four-door BMW sedan made from the early 1960s (in Germany, appearing in Canada in 1966) until 1976, with sweet exhaust note, comfort and speed. Many used to consider it a collector's item. Not the BMW mechanic, however. Its thin-walled aluminum head (which cracks when overheated), twin Solex (**fishing weight**) carbs which pop back and catch fire when out of adjustment...make this car eligible for the stark fist of removal from many a shop. "Say, how much do I have to *pay* not to work on this car, lady?"

bazoo — French-Canadian term for a derelict or just old, beloved car. An early cheap used car rental agency in Montreal was called "Beau Bazou."

bean oil — The one and only Castrol "R", a red, racing type oil known for its ability to protect motors, permanently and completely foul spark plugs, smell wild and exotic, a racing smell. Castor bean oil, the source of Castrol, breaks down at higher temperatures than other oils. It says "organic" on the can. An early reader of this ms. comments: "the smell alone is enough for the true enthusiast to fail the breathalizer test in any jurisdiction."

bear bait — car talk term adapted from CB lingo, where "bears" are police. "Bear bait" is the car that passes you going 75 miles per hour. "There's a bear out there taking pictures." See "taking **pictures on the Pershing."**

bear trap — clutch in Laverda motorcycles, named after amount of effort required to pull clutch lever in, and consequently the way it behaves upon release.

beater — a used car costing, say, $150. —overheard on CHOM, Montreal. The word may be an adaptation of the phrase "old beat-up car", or a sideways short form of "eggbeater," which is what the ticking, clicking, motor often sounds like. "Its heart is still beating, anyways!" See also **bazou, clunker.**

A good definition of "beater" is offered by Doug Sweet in his "Cars" column in the Montréal *Gazette* of February 3, 1990: "An elderly, inexpensive automobile, usually of North American manufacture, equipped with V-8 engine, good battery, excellent heater and a radio. A beater's body is usually dented and at least a little bit rusty. There may be a tail-light lens missing or a piece of bumper hanging off. Beaters are most often seen on Prairie roads in the dead of winter."

One parts man reports hearing "beater" applied to the car used for fetching parts from the other end of a sprawling wrecking yard. The greasy, overalled mechanic bounded into (no door on it), started, gunned it, and shot down a deeply trenched muddy path between other wrecks. It resembled a destruction derby special. It had been a **totaled** vehicle, but someone noticed—"hey, Fred, this one runs pretty good," and after pulling the ruined fenders back off of the tires and suspension and fitting it with wheels of other colors and sizes, they put it to use. Driven like hell, abused, its other functions smashed long ago, its radio usually works.

beaverwood — Toronto slang name for the wood on the old **woodies** which became a part of a punch-your-buddy game: when you spotted a station wagon with wood trim, you would say "Beaverwood, no return" and thus earned the right to punch friend on arm without his or her having the right to punch you back.

bed rocking — in **lowrider** shows, cars and trucks show off their stuff: upholstered trunks, complete with fur, velvet Elvis art, wet bar, etc. One favorite feature is "jumping," using the electric-hydraulic rams in place of shock absorbers. "Bed rocking" is new. Pickup truck lowriders have beds that rock from side to side, using pumps.

beef it — in motorcycle racing, skateboarding, etc., to go down hard enough to scrape the skin off real bad, exposing......"Oh, I see that you beefed it last Sunday." See also **gravel rash.**

beemer — affectionate term for a BMW. According to Erwin Schieder, usually spelled "Bimmer" in *Road and Track* and other car mags, to reflect the more authentic German pronunciation. However, Neil Hancock, sci-fi and fantasy author in Austin Texas and an old biker, reports that the primary meaning for them of "beemer" is "the two-cylinder motorcycle" and that they secretly think "bimmer people" are "yuppie-prick chickenshits who can't usually even change their tires easily, let alone set their own valves or check timing, etc." BMW motorcycle owners can or at least should be able to tune their machines out in the Big Bend desert if necessary.

beemin' — "to drive an automobile designed by BMW. Also (2) to smoke narcotics, namely cocaine. "Yo, check it out, I saw both of them beemin' down 5th avenue yesterday and the car was all repainted!" —From Marvel's *Rap*

Dictionary, 1991, as cited in "You got to be ampin'", *Montreal Gazette*, November 17, 1991.

beercan — jocular term for a Volkswagen, or any small light car that would crumple in almost any collision at any speed.

beetle — starting with 25 horsepower, this Volkswagen was "the best car ever built" in the sense of "best value." It was built for more years than the Model T.

Beezer — BSA motorcycle. B. S. A. stood for Birmingham Small Arms.

belchfire power plant — a term for the motor in "U.S.-built autos from 1967 to 1970", which have a reputation for fairly high reliability and power. —Robert Appel, *The Used Car Believer's Handbook.*

Belisha beacon — British term for **cat's eyes,** the little inserts in the pavement between traffic lanes on a freeway to warn the driver he's wandering.

bells and whistles — optional equipment. See **taco wagon.**

belly up — to die. Also, to roll the car, to turn it over.

bench racing — talking about racing, especially just after an event, according to John Lawlor's *How to talk car.*

Bennett buggy — "a car converted to a four-wheel, horse-drawn carriage by the removal of the engine, the drive train, and windshield (unless the windshield was of the type that opened). Named after R.B. Bennett [Prime Minister of Canada in the 30s], this depression vehicle is better known than the **Anderson cart** but served the same purpose—the utilization of the car chassis that could no longer be used as a car due to the lack of money, gas, parts, or the like. As noted under **Anderson cart** the name reflects the blame that was placed on politicians for the depression. —Chris Thain, in *Cold as a Bay Street Banker's Heart: The Ultimate Prairie Phrase Book* Western Producer Prairie Books, Saskatoon, Sask., 1987.

benzie-box — "a removable car stereo system." from Mercedes-Benz. —From Marvel's *Rap Dictionary*, 1991, as cited in "You got to be ampin'", Montréal *Gazette*, November 17, 1991.

benzina — Italian term for gasoline. See also **petrol.**

benzine — German term for gasoline.

berm shot — motorcycle racing term for catching and passing someone on the ridge thrown up by the racers in the curves, so that they may bank off it and lean as they turn (a "bank shot," as in pool). See also **fallen rider pass.**

Bertone — actually a Fiat. Bertone is the designer, also of Alfa Romeo bodies. Fiat no longer imports into North America in its own name (which is *mud*).

"better idea" — derisive term used for some of Ford's weird under-hood gadgetry (tomato juice can vacuum canisters, etc....) This term was derived from Ford advertising of the 1970s and 80s that backfired.

beware of bargains in brain surgery and brake repair — mechanics' proverb.

big and littles — "usually found on street rods, different height tires, the fronts often 4" less than the rears, causing the car to have a good looking rake or stance." —from Paul Burrill, Madison WI.

big-bore — a machine with an engine in which the pistons work in large cylinders, producing massive power.

big city feeling — to have the benefit of the roaring and pounding of construction equipment (jack hammers, front end loaders, compressor engines, etc.), with your breakfast. See also **Meskin resort feeling.**

Big Daddy — Don Garlits, premier drag racer, driving the "Florida Swamp Rat" (170 mph in a quarter mile, in 1956). Californians didn't believe his claimed speed; they challenged him; he drove out with "Swamp Rat" on a trailer and **shut em down.** Anyone who thinks that drag racing went out in the '60s should be at the front of the pack when the light changes.

big green — "sponsors" —from C. H. B. in the San Antonio *Current* the day before the San Antonio Gran Prix (1988). The color refers to the money they put up.

big motor — in car racing slang, an engine that is illegally oversized.

big slip daddy — a limited slip differential, in the Beach Boys song "Little Deuce Coupe."

big time — buzz word. When you make the big time, you've either

1) won the race, ... 2) crashed, killing yourself or spectators,......or 3) committed some horrible crime and made the news. ("You've fucked up big time, buddy").

bimmer — see **beemer.**

binders — brakes, in car racing slang. Also **anchors** (British, U. K. usage) — as in "throw out the ...."

bing bing — derisive term for small displacement two-stroke motorcycles. Like **wing ding,** they do sound that way, don't they?

birdcage Maserati — driven to success by Stirling Moss in 1956 (race car with ultralight frame consisting of lots of small aluminum tubes with aluminum skin stretched over them.

bird catcher — blower intake that sticks out of the hood.

bird's nest — large, deep, untidy, often ragged hole in bottom of driver's seat, indention left after long use by extra fat person.

bitch pad — Among Hell's Angels in Vancouver, the little seat added above and behind the regular Harley seat on your bike, for guess who to ride on?

to **bite it** — to crash. "He bit it real hard!"

Bitsa Bike — a motorcycle made up of parts from various brands of motorcycle—bits o' this and bits o' that......What do you do with a wrecked MZ motorcycle with a good motor and Triumph 250 with a bad motor? Mate the two. (Photo caption under a Caribbean Bitsa bike in *Classic Bike Magazine,* February 1990).

bi Turbo — two little (or not so little) turbos, depending on the beast. On a 6-cylinder, three per turbo; on a V-8, four per turbo.

black and white — police term for their own **marked car**, or **cruiser.** Black and white were the original universal North American colors for police cars, but the term has stuck even after the colors changed.

black ball — *Consumer Reports'* own symbol of worst rating (good is a circle, very good a red ball, bad a black ball). See classification under Audi for a whole slew of black balls.

black-flagged — in racing, to be ordered off the course by official waving a black flag, for such reasons as leaking oil onto the track, cutting the course, cheating flagrantly, wheel falling off, being on fire and not knowing it, etc. When the black flag is rolled up and pointed at you, it is a warning: "Stop doing that or you *will be* black-flagged." Also known as the **meatball flag.**

black-plate temperature — engineering term for very hot in Texas: "the temperature a metal plate, black, lying in the sun on flat ground with no wind, reaches on a 100 degree Fahrenheit day." About 160 degrees. **White-plate temperature** using the same procedure is about 110. Why, in Texas, you should buy a white rather than a black car.

In Texas, most of the year, it's not which car is fast or flashy. They ask, "Which one has *real cold air conditioning*?"

blacks in big cars — "You can live in yo car, but you can't drive no apartment!"

Black Widow — the limited edition 1957 Chevrolet fuel-injected so that it produced 283 horsepower, matching the horsepower to the 283 cubic inch displacement. The first car banned from stock-car racing.

blind headlight — a headlight in which the reflector (the reflective coating inside the bulb) is starting to corrode.

block head — the new Harley engine, the "evolution" or EVO engine, so called because the heads are block shaped. See also **flat head, pan head, knuckle head, shovel head.**

blocking — "preventing a competitor from passing. It is forbidden, but there has been a lot of it this season." —from C. H. B. in the San Antonio *Current,* the day before the San Antonio Gran Prix (1988). "It never hurts to try." Not allowing a faster competitor to pass. May be warned or **black flagged.**

bloke car — old 60s, 70s MGs, usually loud, fast, twin car rust buckets sold to jet jockey American pilots stationed in England. "I'd like to have a Porsche or BMW," he confides to me, "after I get out, but for here, this bloke car is a hell of a lot of fun to drive, and it was fairly cheap to buy."

don't **blow a gasket** — Steve Poteet's expression for "please cool down." Blowing a gasket is losing it emotionally. "Now don't blow a gasket, lady."

blow beets — to throw up out the window while moving. A.k.a. "hurl," "flash".

Blower Bentley — the most famous 4.5 or 6-litre engined, supercharged car made between the World Wars. Also known as the "Screamer," its noisy, gear-driven compressor of the air-gas mixture "blew" rather than sucking, as modern **turbo superchargers** do. The 6-inch diameter exhaust pipes gave volume to the scream. "Roots" was the name of the type of supercharger.

blowing back the leaves — trucker citizens-band radio talk for "driving fast."

blow in the weeds — to leave someone behind.

blown — dragster having a blower (a supercharger), usually developing in the range of 500 horsepower, with a parachute to stop, fire extinguishers in place under the hood, driver's compartment fitted with a **red handle** for the driver to pull. See also **go or blow.**

A "blown engine" may either mean "turbo or super-charged" (good), or "kaput" (bad).

blow the doors off him — figurative expression describing passing someone going so fast the door of his car may be sucked open.

blue dots — "a blue gem mounted in a taillamp lens causing the lights to have a purple appearance." —from Paul Burrill, Madison WI.

bluehair — a senior bad driver, who makes irrational unexpected stops, doesn't see what's coming, etc. Also **greyhair.**

blue wrench — "Simple," Butch says, "take the blue wrench and get it cherry red, and then it'll come off." The blue wrench is the acetylene torch, from its bright blue flame.

BMW — officially Bayerische Motoren Werke AG, it has also been said that in Boston it means **Break My Window,** and in Montreal, after someone asks how you got to the party, "BMW, bus, metro and walk." The latter has been called a Yuppie joke.

When the letters are pronounced the German way, "Bay emm Vay," the proper rhyme is possible for a German saying, "BMW, Verreckt in Schnee," — "BMW Chokes in Snow."

— aka **B**ig **M**oney **W**aster.

The special reputation of these cars comes from performance, engineering, and handling. It is worth noting that the early Messerschmidts, German fighter air-

craft, like the "Taifun," were partly built by BMW.
B. M. Wobbly — parts men's term. In Europe, especially France and Germany, so many pimps own BMWs, or they are such a status symbol that people think of them as **pimpmobiles**, that one explanation of the acronym in France is "Black Man Wheels." See also **beemer, bimmer.**

boat — a big car, not easy to maneuver if you aren't used to it. See also **land yacht.**

boat tail — Alfa Spyder convertible, named because the rear end comes to a point. An early one, some say the original, was the 1932 Duesenberg Boat Tail Speedster SJ, but the Hispano-Suiza has also been cited for this title. Another example is the 1973 Buick Riviera. See also **disco volante, duetto, camtail.**

Bob Bullock test — to try to find out how fast a BMW will go, among Austin, Texas mechanics, because Bob Bullock, state comptroller of the State of Texas, on the first day he owned a 633 CSI, was stopped for doing 115 mph with beer on his breath, and, after his release by the Department of Public Safety officer, traded it for a 320i, a smaller, not so fast, BMW.

body shop weather — weather which causes "fender benders" (rain, fog, etc.) —from Larry Stafford, owner of "The Dent" body shop. "We love it when it rains."

Bombardier — "Jean-Pierre", pronounced "John Peer," is rhyming slang among some American bike shop blokes for any reference to the Can-Am motorcycle, manufactured originally by this growing young giant in the world of motorized speed vehicles. You can't hear the rhyme unless you say both words the way Americans do: "bombardeer," and "Jean Pierre" as above. André Bombardier, son of the inventor of the snowmobile, works in the corporation headed by his brother-in-law which has within recent years acquired Canadair (aircraft industry: famous for fighter planes and the world's best water bomber, the CL 215, the Challenger corporate jet, and a new regional jet), Short's (Irish/British old aircraft company), Lear, and de Havilland; and from its original snowmobile manufacture has diversified also into subway cars, rolling stock for the Chunnel, etc. And, in fact, before snowmobiles, Bombardier made an electric car. Maybe the boys at the Harley shop feel crowded....

Actually, "Jean-Pierre" is the derisive nickname given to the Can-Am, the Bombardier motorcycle, a "big, clumsy, single pistoned dirt bike that didn't quite make it in the US/Canadian motocross-enduro market...." —from Steve Tufts at Cycle Salvage in Austin TX, who sees the whole derelict bunch eventually, bless his heart. An, ahem, spokesman for Bombardier who asked that his name not be used comments that the Can-Am was "a highly successful 'must-have' for those playing to win. Powered by Rotax engine (like the Skidoos) — Rotax is also owned by Bombardier — the Can-Am is now built by Harley-Davidson ! as a military bike for the U. S. Army and the U. K." He does acknowledge that it was a trifle expensive.

Bondo mechanic — lowest form of bodyworker. Not an artist, he slops on big gobs of body putty to fix dents rather than pounding them out. This shoddy work is made possible by the use of a layer of Bondo to finish the edges.

bone dome — British slang expression for **skid lid.**

bonnet — the hood, in British usage. Simon Petzold, of Montréal, has pointed out that British and American usage in car and railroad terms are very different (a "boxcar" is a "goods' waggon" in England; a "caboose" a "guard's-van.") Aviation terms, on the other hand, tended to be much more uniform between the two Allies.

booger picker — (for those who don't know, a "booger" in the Southwest is nose-pickings) a long, screwdriver-handled pick with the tip bent over and curved to the side, used to extract cotter pins, old oil seals, and install windshields.

to **book** — to "peel off," "peel out," or drive very fast.

boom car — car with grossly oversized sound system (*Austin American-Statesman,* describing 6th Street Saturday night).

boost — "the amount of air a turbocharger is delivering to the engine. Everyone wants more." —from C. B. H. in the San Antonio *Current* the day before the San Antonio Gran Prix (1988). "In IMSA racing, a driver cannot control the boost from the cockpit, but it can be adjusted by the pit crew. IMSA rules also require a restrictor plate on the turbo intake which limits boost." —from CHB. The measure of intake manifold pressurization (see **boost gauge**) which the turbocharger is putting out in lbs/square inch.

the boot — the trunk, in British usage.

bootlegger's turn — a high-speed U-turn. The *Dictionary of American Regional English* defines it as "a method of reversing a vehicle's direction," with the illustration "backing across the other lane of the road, then going forward."

boots — jocular term for unusually large, oversize tires. Also **sneakers.** "They sure put a set of boots on that one!" In British usage, also the protective leather covers over leaf springs.

bored — having the motor cylinder interior reamed, ground out, to a larger size. Increases size of the displacement, and therefore, you hope, the power available. See also **stroked.** These modifications are often done together—an engine is "bored and stroked."

Borgward Isabella convertible — small, cute German car. Fun and fast (had overhead cam in the 1950s). Extinct. Won the Pan Americana Carrera road race in the early 1950s (Guatemala to El Paso, TX), the last of the old road races, 2500-3000 miles. Other winners, other years, were Lincoln and Hudson.

bottle-fed — setup used to test run an engine on test stand when no fuel pump/fuel tank is present. Refers to bottle of gasoline and rubber hose running down to carburetor.

Botts dots — little bumps built into the pavement to mark the lanes on freeways, to alert careless, drowsy or drunk drivers when they wander at high speed. Named after the inventor, an engineer at UCLA. See also **drunk bumps, city titties, cat's eyes, penguins, Belisha beacons, reading Braille** and **rumble strips, zip strips.**

Boxer Twin — slang term for those beautiful symmetrical twin cylinder BMW motorcycles made in Berlin. It's their symmetry that makes for the rivalry with the new "K" BMW motorcycle model which they call the **flying brick.**

bra — "nose mask, a cloth or plastic cover for the front end of a car, shielding the bumper and grill, with holes for the lights and front license plate, reputedly providing resistance to radar tracking." From "Among the New Words," *American Speech* (1990). Also known as **nose bra, car bra, stealth auto bra, stealth car bra.**

brain bucket — motorcycle crash helmet. See also **skid lid, bone dome.**

those **brake lights** — coming on as the cars ahead of you crest the hill should tell you that there's a radar trap just over the hill. You don't always need a radar detector when you are in a pack of cars.

brassiere en cuir — "brassiere in leather", the Quebec (French) expression for the (vinyl?) flexible cover for the front of your sports or fancy car to keep winter slush and salt off. Sexy, eh? Also rumored to reduce the radar signal bounced back to the police radar trap machine, though how well this works is questionable.

break it loose — spectacularly to interrupt the perfect adhesion of rubber to the road so integral to high-performance motoring, whether by going too fast around a corner, **barking the tires,** or decisively accerating to win a road race. **Breaking the wheels loose.**

breaker — British slang for "wrecker," the jobber who buys derelict or nonfunctioning cars and sells them as parts.

Brit — jocular term for any English car.

British racing green — see **National racing colors.**

B. R. M. — British Racing Machine. Builder of lots of kinds of formula racing cars, including the first H-16 1 1/2 litre (small piston) race motor. A fan of long standing comments: "It was supercharged. It had the most adrenaline-boosting scream I've ever heard from anything. I would literally come up on tiptoe and stop breathing. Of course, the sound didn't last long. Usually preceded a bang."

brodie — "I suddenly cranked the wheel hard-left and spun the Caddy through a full 360^0, your classic brodie." —from Jim Dodge's *Not Fade Away* (New York: Atlantic Monthly Press, 1987), a latter-day "On the Road" book with car talk throughout.

broken kitty — Jaguar. From an ad in *Car and Driver* of September 1988. A case of clever advertising picking up a piece of the people's car talk. "Broken" refers as much to "breaking a mustang" as to "housebroken." Ever try to "housebreak" a jaguar?

Brooklands racer — eventually applied to identify a kind of British racing car of the 1930s and 40s, the term comes from the name of an old industrial area racetrack south of London with banked turns and long straightaways, approximately oval in shape overall. The race track was old, dating from near the turn of the century, but its singularity emerged during the 1930s because of the experimentation with aircraft engine technology. The track enclosed a flying field. Near the Riley aircraft engine factory, it was the site of races between Napier and Railton race cars, the former powered by the Rolls-Royce, Lion V-12 and H-24 engines (also used as the Lancaster bomber engine), and the Rolls Merlins, with 24-cylinder supercharged engines also used in the Spitfire fighter aircraft. Some were V-12s: the Lancasters developed 1100 horsepower. The Indy 500 of England. See also **Allison V-12.**

bubble car — see **go-go-mobile.**

Buckaroo Banzai — the 8th dimension cult film of go-fast bad boys. Buckaroo, aided by mad scientist type from "Back to the Future," tests theory that if you go fast enough on dry ground, you enter the eighth dimension. Buckaroo's Ford van is supercharged, nitrous-oxide injected, fast California speed shop best.

Upon opening the hood of a really nicely set up performance BMW 2002 with dual Weber carbs, we have overheard the following exclamation : "Ripper Bipper Buckaroo Bonzai!"

The word "banzai" is a car term older than the movie: John Lawlor's *How to talk car* defines it as "all-out effort," and says that "a competitor who pushes his car to the absolute limit during a drag race is making a banzai run." Going right back to the beginning, "BANZAI" was the cry of the Kamikaze pilots as they dived.

Bugatti — made between 1918 and 1930s, by Ettore Bugatti, double overhead cam, two straight-8s in solid block (no head, no head gasket) engines had to be serviced for major repairs by coming in from underneath. The Bugatti Royale was largest passenger car of the time, and maybe, excluding the "stretch limos", of all time, at 22 feet or so loooong. Only seven built. Ettore Bugatti said, of starting problems with his cars, "anyone rich enough to own one is also rich enough to afford a heated garage." —from Don Hackett. In April 1990 a 59 year-old Bugatti Royale sold for $16.38 million, setting a record (the previous high was $15.21 million for a 1963 Ferrari GTO in November 1989.

bugeye — the Austin-Healy Sprite. Small, fun 4-cylinder convertible. In England, called the "frogeyed sprite." Extinct.

bug juice — "Have it your way, lady," Artie says, exasperated. "I'll raise the dam idle if you want." (Bends over car, adjusts idle with a screwdriver.) "Do you want a dragonfly in it too?" he asks, picking the dragonfly off the grille. He manually throttles the engine up. A look of horror on her face as Artie drops the insect down the throat of the carb. The little Renault engine hisses for a second, then roars. "Does it really help?" she asks, quietly. "It lubricates the valves," Artie says. Bug juice.

Buick — Back in the good ole' days, these cars were so lush and grand in an overblown sort of way that they have entered college slang of the 1980s-90s to describe "throwing up": "to ride the Buick" and "to sell Buicks," take their place beside "to spill the blue groceries" and "ralph" ("talk to Ralph on the big white phone" is the elaborate form). —Gordon Monson, "Talked to ralph..." (syndicated from the *Los Angeles Daily News*), *Montreal Gazette* (February 10, 1990).

bullet — a fast car.

bullet headlights — bullet-shaped headlights that were mounted prominently on top of the fenders in cars in the late 1930s.

bullet-nose — old Studebaker Champion (body by Ghia) with protruding nose in middle of grille. (Artie painted the nose, on his, orange and affixed a spinner-propeller to it).

bulletproof — said of gearboxes which, having been gone through, race-tested, modified, etc., can be shifted hard, **flogged**, without breaking. The Borg-Warner four-speed gearbox in the early Corvette was one example. Also said of engines. Even the pedestrian Chrysler 2.2 is called this, probably because Shelby goosed it with a turbo for the Omni GLH and kept the bottom end/gearbox etc.,

and they gave a 5 year/ 50,000 mile warranty.
Bullitt — Steve McQueen's famous car chase film, lots of definitive stunt driving in San Francisco.

bum fuck nowhere — "Honey, I've broken down in the middle of **bum fuck nowhere."** See **Clayton NM.**

bumpsteer — "A flaw in the handling of a car after the steering or suspension has been modified. After hitting a bump, the movement of the suspension causes the car to steer one way or another." —from Paul Burrill, Madison WI.

bump start — starting a motorcycle by pushing it, and when it is rolling, popping out the clutch, making the forward inertia turn the engine till it **catches.** A racing motorcycle weighing 400 lbs, with a high compression engine, has to be cranked hard to make the compression necessary to make it fire. So the "bump" is that moment when the clutch is let out, the throttle is dumped, the weight lands on the rear wheel, and the fire makes the bike take off, at high speed, almost immediately. The driver might have to shift, brace himself on the handlebars, and do a sort of horizontal hand-stand to manoeuvre his legs and torso astride of the bike, while keeping the throttle wide open and avoid hitting other racers, all at the same moment! See also **dead start.** Not to be confused with **jump start,** which is done stationary, and with cables. When you "bump start" or "roll start" a car, it's called "pushing it to start." People (like Lewis) who have owned '50 Fords thirty years later, with original 6-volt electrical systems, know how to do this, from much experience.
Don't try this with a BMW motorcycle; it unscrews the drive shaft.

burn off — to start from a stop rapidly by racing the motor and popping out the clutch, causing the drive wheels to spin, making noise and leaving rubber marks on the pavement. Also known as **light up the tires.** Also **burn out, peel out, lay rubber.**

burn the yellow — Montreal term for racing through a yellow light. An English phrase almost exactly translated from a French phrase, actually French from France: "brule le feu," burn the light. The French have another phrase for the same maneuver: "mort la ligne jaune," "kill the yellow line." Traditionally in Montreal, drivers both "burn the yellow" and "jump the green." It is not hard to imagine what this custom does to insurance rates. Color images express the excitement of driving in France. When a light turns green, French drivers make "l'onde vert," "the green wave," roaring away from it in a pack.

It is not only in France that we find a different attitude to traffic lights than is customary in North America. "Luciano De Crescenzo, a Naples-born writer who lives in Rome, says that a red light in his home town is not a command but an opinion. 'Green lights are warnings to drive with caution,' he added. 'Yellow lights? Those we keep for gaiety.'" —Clyde Haberman, "Italian love for cars turning to heartache." Toronto *Globe and Mail* (Oct. 11, 1988), p. A8.

There is actually evidence that these driving habits do exist here and there, now and then, in the United States, too. Jacqueline Baum reports from Boston that when a light turns red there, the next two cars go through the intersection, and "the third car has the option."

burro bars — see **cow catcher, tumba burros.**

bury the tach — to **rev** an engine up to past redline and beyond.

bust ass — a way of describing a difficult mechanic job: "I busted ass getting that one to work!"

butane rig — car, usually from California, with means of burning both gasoline (a bad boy gas burner) and, by flipping a couple of switches, butane. In California, exhaust gas analysis and emission controls checks are performed at roadblocks on the highway. So when the **bad boy** sees a roadblock, he switches to butane, a very clean burning fuel. Butane burns so clean it can be used in enclosed places where humans breathe the air also (e. g. frozen fish plant forklift runs on butane).

to **buy the farm** — often shortened to "he bought it", it means "to die." Adapted from or at least first used in aviation, and before that, from the language of poor sharecroppers, no doubt.

buzzing the motor — "overrevving the engine, a good way to drop a lot of bucks."

C

cabriolet — "European term for convertible," according to John Lawlor's *How to talk car* (1965). Our research seems to corroborate, especially for France and Germany. It is also used in Italy, but in alternation with "convertible." "A roadster or convertible with roll up windows rather than side curtains": —from Paul Burrill, Madison WI.

CAD — computer assisted design. Enabled GM and others to design/engineer shitboxes like the Chevette with a distributor which, in order to service at all, required the mechanic to first unbolt and remove the air conditioner compressor (way to go, boys.)

Caddy — Cadillac.

Cadillac commie — professed left-winger who drives a big car. Same as a **limousine liberal,** in a way.

Cadillac Ranch — see **out to pasture.**

cafe racer — a flashy motorcycle, because they're parked outside of pizza parlors and the like to impress members of the opposite sex. A **crotch rocket.** —from Leonard Zwilling, staff, *Dictionary of American Regional English.*

CAFE — Corporate Average Fuel Economy, "the average mileage for all the cars sold by each automaker. U. S. federal law requires that every automaker's fuel economy average 27.5 mpg for all domestic cars it sells in a year, and, separately, for all imported cars." —Montreal Gazette, Jan. 10, 1991.

California cars — car lovers' state. ("We don't care how they do it in California!") But in all truth, maybe the car performance capital of America. Lots of high-tech shops and equipment manufacturers, of turbochargers, reprogrammed engine computers, performance modified equipment, headers, etc. etc. California has the most cars too....You can't get past 50 mph on the crowded freeways most of the time.

California rolling stop — "You didn't come to a complete stop back there," the cop was saying, ticket book already out and at the ready.

"But officer," she pleaded, "I thought the California rolling stop was legal here in Texas."

"Ahem," he began, "ma'am," taking a deep breath and puffing his chest out, "you can tell that to the judge....but I can tell you what he'll say."

"What's that, officer?" she asks.

"Well, we don't care how they do it in Cal-i-for-ni-a."

See **rolling stop.**

camel jockey — any Iranian, Iraqi, or for that matter any Arabic driver of any vehicle. Also used for parking lot attendants, who are associated with wild driving, backing up fast, etc.

cammy — an engine is "cammy" if it has much more power at certain rpms. See **come on the cam, peaky.**

camtail — Newer Alfa convertible, so named because of its chopped off tail. Should probably be spelled Kamm-tail, from the professor of the same name who developed it in the wind tunnel, but it isn't. See also **boattail, disco volante, duetto.**

Can-Am — A race, to be sure, a class of racing, in fact; but in the motorcycle world, see **Bombardier.**

cannibalized — crippled, deliberately disconnected, e. g. electrical system, for repairs.

cannonball — an unofficial road race, illegal road rally. As in "Cannonball Run", "Cannonball Rally."

carburetor — obsolete. Used to be a part of a car. Now it is a hippie term for a roll of cardboard perforated, joint is inserted and lit, hand is placed over open end, and smoke is inhaled from other end. You release the hand over the end for the "carburetor" effect. From Cheech and Chong, "Pass me that carburetor!"

be **careful with it** she says, handing me the keys to her antique Triumph, "it doesn't like to be moved."

carjacking — a new word for an increasingly terrifying new crime in U. S. cities: stealing a car which is in use, at gunpoint. "[It is difficult to steal] new, expensive cars, most of which are equipped with theft-proof ignition switches and alarm systems. It is much easier to make off with such a vehicle if you also can get the key." Toronto *Globe and Mail,* September 16, 1992.

car keyed — "Someone car keyed my Volvo," Ed says, "in the parking lot at work....probably one of the girls at the office I haven't fucked......" A deliberate act, performed casually while walking along....car key is drawn along side of the car's paint work, scratching a long thin line down the side of the car.

el **carro** — also Mexican name for car (beside el **coche**). Improper Spanish, but millions of gringos adding "o" to American words have had their way. E. g. "El Carro Viejo," restaurant-bar in San Antonio.

Carson top — "Cut the top of a sedan, build a metal framework top, lower than original, cover with cloth. Looks like a convertible top, but does not fold. Usually removable." —from Paul Burrill, Madison WI.

carucha — from Chicano slang, a favorite old car. From Frank Zappa's "Primer me carucha, Chevy '39/ Going to El Monte/ Legion Stadium,/ Pick up on my guisa/ She is so divine/ Helps me stealing hub caps/ Wasted all the time/ Fuzzy dice/ Bongos in the back/ My ship of love is ready to attack." —from Leonard Zwilling, staff, *Dictionary of American Regional English.*

casi nuevo — "I fixed the hood instead of replacing it," the Mexican body man says, "and look at it....casi nuevo, eh?" ('just like new') — another example of the mix of Spanish and English in Southern U. S. car talk......

catch — when a motor is being **cranked over,** when it finally fires and shows signs of wanting to start, you say it **catches.** In Cumberland County, Nova Scotia, a motor that won't "catch", "won't **dog,**" a use of the word that makes sense, because what the starter catches on are metal "dogs" or "lugs."

playing **catch-up** — wild driving, especially on a race-course, when the lead racer has spun out or temporarily lost the lead. Wild and crazy driving, passing lots of cars at once, four-wheel slides, etc.

cat pisser — windshield washers. In South Texas and California, the (often Chicano) **lowriders** will sometimes reverse the sprayer on the cat pissers so they can spray pedestrians who get too close to the machine.

cat's eyes — little reflective bumps set into the pavement on urban freeways to warn drivers who wander out of their lane. Heard in North America, this is the British preferred slang term. See also **Botts dots, drunk bumps, city titties, penguins, zip strips, rumble strips.**

cat-walk — pulling (popping) a **wheelie** on a bicycle or motorcycle and holding it, riding on one (the rear) wheel.

center punching — spectacular accident where one car rams the other in the middle of the side. A term from races at figure-8 racetracks, where such accidents are not only possible but expected by the crowd. Also known as **T-boning.**

chair — motorcycle sidecar. See also **sidehack, trainer wheel.**

chalk-man — police photographer who comes out and chalks the outlines of the fallen before removal.

to do a **Challenger** — to blow up and burn, ever since the NASA Challenger disaster.

chaloupe — Quebec word for "big boat" in the sense of "a wide, heavy usually American car." Also known as a **Yank tank, snowbanker, minoune, land yacht, pig.** The word "chaloupe" is of course the French word from which is derived "shallop," a fairly old English word for a small boat; thus the Quebec use is a jocular diminutive.

Chapman lock — antitheft device in use in New York City which, activated by a switch under the dash, locks the hood and shuts off the gas (probably by disabling the fuel pump) or ignition. The sort of equipment owners are reluctant to describe to strangers in detail, and which mechanics occasionally have to dismantle to get the car to run again. Named for Colin Chapman, who designed it for the Lotus, such a valuable car that it needed such heavy security.

char — Quebecois word for "car," familiar and affectionate. Echoes "chariot." Quebec "retour du chariot" is computer talk for "carriage return." "Si j'avais un char, ca changerait mon vie!" ("If I had a car, it"d change my life......")

A common Quebec French expression for "a truckload" of anything, especially "merde" (bullshit), is "un char en palette," i. e. a "forklift truck with a pallet full of it." "Mangez d'la merde un char en palette!" ("Eat a forklift full of shit!"

How to keep from getting **cheated** at a mechanic you don't know:

1) carry a gun

2) don't talk, don't say words, just grunt and point at the proble; seize the mechanic by his shirt, at the neck, in front, when you point

3) piss on the wall as you leave

A more respectable bit of advice on this subject is offered by Mike Fox and Steve Smith in *Rolls -Royce: The Complete Works (The best 599 Stories about the World's Best Car* : "An anonymous Italian owner ... in 1948 ... wishing to make some modifications to his car, commissioned a seance to call up the spirit of Henry Royce.....The advice from beyond the veil was: 'Consult your authorized distributor.'"

(The "RR" logo on the car, originally silver, became black, one "R" at a time, when Rolls and Royce died.)

cheater — length of pipe or pry bar, slipped over pipe wrench in order to add leverage. "With this cheater, I could move the world if I could find a place to stand."

checkered flag — waved at the finish line of a race. See **black flag.**

checkered sports coat award — mythical award for selling a **dog** sports car for twice its value. "Checkered" also refers to its owner's moral and ethical values. See also **full Cleveland.**

cheese — Bondo, a plastic body-fill compound. See **Bondo mechanic.**

cheese-covered roller skate — a term for tiny cars, e. g. the Honda 600. Mini-cars.

cherry — light on top of a cop car. See also **gumball machine, firecracker.**

— a complimentary term for a car in brand-new, perfect condition, "virgin." **Cream puff.**

— a model name, overseas, for the Datsun F10.

cherry bomb muffler — also known as the **glass-pack**, but painted red for hotrodders. Later rather elongated, they were at first bulbous, like the famous firecracker. See also **Smittys.**

cherrypicker — an engine hoist. The more generally known denotation for this term is "a chair-hoist on a truck to raise a worker to the level needed to work on a power line, a power pole, or a street light."

chevy eleven — used car term for the Chevy II, predecessor of the Nova.

chicane, chicaine (Montreal spelling) — an S curve in a race track. "Any squiggle on a track which tends to slow the car down, such as a right turn followed quickly by a left." —from CHB. From the French for "a deceptive maneuver, a move to make interception elusive," and before that, from Persian "chugan," a game which is an ancestor of hockey. The words "bandy" and "chicanery" both come from the world of stickball, for such moves. See Lewis and Aaron Poteet, *The Hockey Word Book,* Hantsport, N.S.: Lancelot Press, 1991). See also **moving chicane.** Designed in the 1930s to slow down race cars on the long straightaways in the Monaco Gran Prix, etc., with the result that in 1954, Alberto Ascari took his Lancia Ferrari over the sea wall in a spectacular wipeout.

In Montreal, a well-known "chicaine" leading into the final straightaway at Le Circuit Gilles Villeneuve on Ile Notre Dame was to be replaced during 1989 by "two 90-degree right-to-left turns" to slow down the drivers, who had been charging through the chicaine at up to 240 kph, according to Ian MacDonald of the *Gazette* (February 4, 1989). The effect, besides safety, will be to give spectators in the grandstand better views of the cars and drivers.

Chicago screwdriver — a hammer.

Chicanomobile — a derogatory term in areas of the United States with lots of Latinos, for a car with fluffy interior, tassels, **low-rider** equipment, etc. A **taco wagon.**

chicharon — colloquial Mexican for "toasted," as in fried pork rinds, etc. Said in awe, with emphasis on "ron", for "burned to a cinder," of spectacular burnups....drag racers going end over end in flames, Challenger, etc.

chicken — a sort of automotive Russian roulette played especially during the 1950s in which two drivers would race toward each other at top speed, each with one wheel over the white centerline, to see which one would veer away first and thus show himself to be "chicken," i. e. not courageous. Sometimes neither one would, and both drivers would be turned into hamburger, and the two cars into scrap metal. Another way to play the game, with two really terminal old cars, was to race them toward a cliff and see who jumped out of the car last.

Chinese fire drill — when everybody gets out of the car at a stop light and runs around it, getting back in before light changes. Lots of squealing. Teenager car game. See also **punch buggy, beaverwood.**

chingadera — Spanish for "goddam thing," a name for any object you can't remember the right name for. Same as **clyde, thingamajigger, doomaflockie, chingaso, frammis, whatchamacallit.**

chinger — to mar a surface, as in using pliers to turn a nut, thus rounding off the corners. From Spanish "chinga," "to fuck" ("the bolts on this car are all chingered up.")

chisel-back Cadillac — later on (1981-85) model Cadillac Seville had this style, which is a throwback style to an old Rolls or something made for less trunk space. It looks like a chisel!

Chitwood brothers — Joie and Tim, stuntmen in the movies and commercials who get the car up on two wheels, and balance it while they drive it through various openings too narrow for a car to fit through with four wheels on the ground. Automotive specialist stunt men.

choke — on late-model cars, practically obsolete term, with fuel injection and all. New meaning: when your football team loses steam, and starts getting clobbered. It "chokes."

choir practice — cops cutting up, out by themselves. — from Joseph Wambaugh's *The Choir Boys*. Local Austin cops had a little dirt track off of Spicewood Springs Road where they used to race their police cruisers around.

chop shop — where car thieves **strip** stolen cars.

chopped and **channeled** — especially in the 1950s, a way of modifying a car to make it look sexy. Suspension would be changed to lower the car; and a section would be taken out of the windows and roof-posts (chopping) to lower and make the windows look longer. The car would hug the road like a Hudson Hornet, or look like it would. A similar, less extensive modification was the **chopped top.**

chopper — heavily modified motorcycle with long forks, and a solid rear suspension (**hardtail**). Early style choppers (remember the movie "Easy Riders"?) with long, high forks were a bitch to drive at low speeds, were apt to fail structurally at bad holes in road, and caused many cops to see red. Later on Harley Davidson built a model, the Sturgis, with some fork extension, sturdy, with 80 cubic inches, fast and powerful, and with none of the handling problems of earlier chopped bikes. (Sturgis, South Dakota, is the site of the annual Harley bike meet).

Christmas Tree — starting lights at a drag strip.

tout **chromé** — Quebec French expression to describe a car with a heavily chromed and clean engine.

chrome plated and updated — rhyming slang car talk. "A good design doesn't need to be chrome plated and updated." See also **power brake and jet off-take.**

Church of Divine Transmission Repair — East Austin, Tex. There is a waiter at a certain Mexican restaurant who, faced with crisis, prayed for and was delivered from problems (slippage, I think) with his 1953 Chevy Belair. He has since prayed for other cars in his community, with some success. Resisting efforts to go commercial, Manuel prays still, he says, "when I'm having trouble."

Honda "City" — tiniest model of Honda, not sold in America. Big enough for one driver and two bags of groceries. "**Cheese-covered roller skate**."

city lights — low-beam headlights, as they were known in Milwaukee, during the 1930s, according to the *Dictionary of American Regional English.* See also **duck lights.**

city titties — those little bumps set in the pavement to define traffic lanes. Also known as **drunk bumps** (you hit them more when drinking.) See **reading Braille, Botts dots, rumble strips, zip strips.**

class action suit — what you join in, with aid from your lawyer, in order to sue car manufacturers for mass-produced defects.

classic — According to John Lawlor's *How to talk car*, mostly 1930s and 1940s luxury cars are called by this name, but, acknowledging that "the dates aren't absolutely firm," he mentions the original Lincoln Continental (1948), and with the progress of time, 1950s cars are now looking like classics, and if they're in top shape, costing that much, too. Don Hackett fixes the terminal date for the "classic" (in 1988) at 1963, with the Studebaker Avanti.

Clayton, NM — name synonymous with both **vapor lock** and **bum fuck nowhere.** Little town about 60 miles out of Albuquerque, high and hot—temperatures above 110 degrees Fahrenheit are common here, and this heat, combined with the high altitude, cause loads of vehicles to boil their fuel (either in the fuel lines, fuel pump, or carburetor) and shut down, until you figure out how to shut the air conditioner off, cool the thing down, pour a beer over the fuel pump, or remove the car hood and drive with it off.

Clayton is a town of gas stations and tow truck drivers, so there is rescue, at a price. See **bum fuck nowhere.**

tell me when I'm **clean** — i. e. when it's safe to pull out into traffic.

clean the clock — score an overwhelming victory, set a new record, etc., in racing.

clean the shaft — **strip** the gears, i. e. releasing the clutch too quickly with the motor running at high revolutions per minute (rpm) and changing gears, breaking teeth off the spline shaft. Inexperienced drivers are more likely to do this, trying to **burn rubber** (which see). A Nova Scotia jocular interjection when someone is in danger of cleaning the shaft, grinding the gears, is "Grind a pound for me." In the U. K. it is "Can you play 'God Save the King'?"

Clear Hooters — name of English company, originally the only manufacturer of horns. Name ends up on head light switches, horn relays, etc. Competitors to Joseph Lucas, **Prince of Darkness** and in the U. K., **Inventor of Night.**

clencher — In Quebec French, part of a memorable proverbial instruction: "Il ne faut pas clencher tout suite!" (Don't grab a handful right away—in other words, warm it up before you open it up). —from Nicolas Poteet.

click over — during an attempt to start a car, this condition is worse than if it will actually **crank over;** in this case, the solenoid only produces a clicking sound, but the starter is not able to turn the engine over.

clicks — kilometers. "I put on ten thousand klicks at least since I last changed the oil in her!" Originally from Army talk, as it used metric maps.

clips — hold many parts *to* your car. Not paper clips, but in some way kin.

over two hundred thousand miles **on the clock** — on the car. The clock suggests the odometer, from which the exact total mileage is read, unless it is over a hundred thousand, in which case you have to know how many times it has gone around.

clocked — "I clocked you doing 75 back there, boy." Old fashioned alternative to modern radar. Clocking is measuring your rate of speed by 1) timing you going between two highway stripes, a pre-measured distance, 2) following you in unmarked or marked car and comparing your speed to patrol car's speed. "Why you were going as fast as I was, officer, sir." "Makes no difference, boy, I was catching you."

closet dead person — e. g. a young frat boy wearing only tennis shoes, gym shorts, and sunglasses, tearing down a 30 mph street on his big fast motorcycle at 100 mph. "He's dead," a bystander says, "he just hasn't come out of the closet yet." See **organ transplant.**

clunker — a really abused, defective old car. The name is highly descriptive, because driving one of these that will run produces loud, disturbing sounds from motor, transmission, and/or running gear.

clutch start — a standing, not rolling start in a motorcycle race. As in drag race, from a grid, in gear, with engine running. See also **Le Mans start, hand on helmet start, wave start, dead start.**

clyde — name for any object you can't remember the name of. Also **doomaflockie, thingamajigger,** and in Mexico and California (Chicano), **chingadera, chingaso.**

CO — carbon monoxide. Inevitable gas component of engine exhaust fumes, odorless, deadly. Why you don't warm the car up in the garage.....

cobbing it on — grabbing a big handful of throttle (motorcycle). Stuffing your foot into it (automobile). The movement of the hand, twisting the grip, reveals the origin of the term: it's the gesture you make when you're shucking or eating a piece of corn on the cob.

el **coche** — Mexican name, proper Spanish, for "automobile." See el **carro.**

cog — British term for "gear." "I grabbed the bottom cog," means "I slapped it into bottom, or first, gear").

colors — a garment, usually a t-shirt or jacket worn by a club member. Among car people, "you bring a t-shirt and we all get to piss on it and then you have to wear it and you can never wash it again, and after *that* we'll have a regular blood initiation and everything." —from the movie American Graffitti.

come aboard of me — Newfoundland way to say "ran into me." Adapted from nautical talk.

come on the cam — engines with racing cams typically have less power than a normal engine at low revs, but then they come on the cam at some higher speed, say 4000 rpm. Then it's like being fired from a cannon. An engine with this type of behaviour is also called **cammy** or **peaky.** The opposite is an engine with **low-end grunt.**

commie — any car manufactured in the Eastern Bloc countries, i. e. Yugo, Lada, MZ, Skoda, etc. "Mister, get that commie piece a shit outa here!"

coming on the pipe, coming on song — to accelerate a perfectly **tuned-up** engine to the point where the balance is productive of a sound musical to the right ear.

committed — going so fast that one is committed to a line (going through the corner). From ESPN commentary on SCAA racing. (Race track had an escape road in mid-corner, but .....)

como dios manda — he had already fixed the flat and was crawling out from under the truck, having tightened the spare tire onto its carrier.

"Is it ready?" I asked. "Si," he answers. "Is the spare tightened real good?" I ask. "Si, como dios manda," he answers. ["as God commands"]

Used in this way, the phrase expresses both extreme devotion to duty, particularly important in dealing with potentially dangerous procedures in mechanics work if neglected, and also suggests that the customer is *God.* An infusion of Spanish into Southern U. S. car talk.....

company cars — "don't need anything but gas and oil, you know." Said by an Austin car parts deliveryman to explain why his car, supplied by the store, is in less than perfect repair.

concours d'elegance — show or contest of vehicles and accessories in which entries are judged chiefly on excellence and appearance (wash the underside of that Jaguar, bub).

a **cooking engine** — may mean "an engine that's really **cooking**," as below, or by analogy with "cooking sherry," a plain engine, for sedans, which has to be made hotter with modifications for sports car performance or racing. I. e. the two meanings are opposite. —Tom Brown.
cooking your engine — from the U. K., blowing it up, **overrev**ving it, etc.
cooking on your car engine — a new book of 1989 is Chris Maynard and Bill Scheller's *Manifold Destiny: The One, the Only Guide to Cooking On Your Car Engine*, with recipes and cooking times. Actually, instead of times, the cooking is specified by number of miles, for specific engines: e. g. it takes 55 miles to reheat stuffed cabbage on a V-8.

Coon Tosh — spelling to indicate pronunciation of the name of the Lamborghini Countach, the "ultimate exotic" car according to John McPhee in the Dec. 4, 1989 *New Yorker*.

cop 'stang — a police Ford Mustang. Often equipped with headers and bigger four-barrel carburetors, and possibly a 351 engine instead of the stock 302.

corkscrew — descending tight turn....indefinable, but .... means you don't have to drive the world's fastest or most powerful car, to have fun. Power-to-weight ratio is the key. A light small car may have a better power-to-weight ratio than a large one (Porsche, Sprite, hot VW, etc.) See **fun factor.**

cornering on the door handles — figurative, not literal expression. Fast cornering, especially in TV movies (American sedans lean a lot in the corners). "Scraping the door handles." "I rode to lunch with someone who did this, and now I won't ride anywhere with him." **Doorhandling it.**

cosmoline — yellowish waxy rustproof coating on new cars, brake drums, rotors, chrome pieces.

couch and carry plan — a way to pay for car repairs, by exchanging sex for work. Especially made available by the (mostly) male mechanics for attractive female customers. Largely a greaseball's fantasy!

coupe — a two-door, short wheelbase car with small windows on both sides for the rear seat. The word is French for "cut."

course cutting — illegally cutting off part of course for personal gain of distance. Penalty: **black flagging**, at the very least.

cover the eye of the bull — a term from bullfighting, used to describe grinning and waving at the cop.

like a **cow pissing on a flat rock** — another memorable Texas saying which describes the way thin liquids (like hot antifreeze) go sideways when they're poured out.

cowboy Cadillac — a pickup.

cow catcher — the grille guard on a pickup or big truck. Also known as **burro bars, deer catcher, roo bars.** The term originally comes from the grillework on the front of steam locomotives, in the early days of railroading.

cram it, ram it, and rotate it — similar to **yell and hit it,** an idiot's method of automotive repair.

whatever turns your **crank** — a Nova Scotia way to say "whatever you like, whatever gets you going enthusiastically." One of many adaptations from car talk of this word, which often stands for the male sex organ in male talk.

cranking over — during starting, "cranking over" refers to the starter's actually turning the engine over, without the ignition catching so that the motor actually runs. See **click over.**

crash box — nonsynchromesh gear box. —U. K.

crayola — parts men's term for the Toyota Corolla.

crazed — technical term for lots of minute surface cracks on face of flywheels, clutch pressure plates — caused by lots of use.....if not *too* deep, can be machined down to good metal.....unless you own a low tolerance machine such as BMW, where it is recommended you replace the part.

cream puff — a perfect, attractive automobile. See **cherry.**

creeper — wooden platform on low casters built to enable mechanic to slip beneath car. Equipped with a little cushion for your head. They are quite comfortable. An ex-mechanic (now a boss), friend of mine went to sleep on his creeper under a large car, with feet sticking out. Noticing that he wasn't moving, a friend yanked him out by his feet....look of total surprise on sleeper's face as he is whirled into glaring daylight. "I was dreaming already," he says.

crotch rocket — the new breed of Ninka, Kawasaki X-11, Yamaha FZR, etc. —track (racing) bikes with lights, flashers (turn signals) and mirrors!

crowd killer — a three-seat station wagon.

crownwheel — British term for "differential ring gear."

crudium — the shit you scrape off vital motor parts/ oil pan leavings, etc. "Uh, lots of crudium under yer car, sir." "There's crudium in your fuel injection......." Aka "gra-doo."

cruelty to a motor scooter — imaginary traffic offense. When you see obvious overloading. This happens a lot. Each one of those little scooters has a little tag that says how much the driver/rider may weigh (usual maximum 150 lbs. on Vespa 50, Honda, etc.). The little tires are squished by overweight riders.

cruise and collect — "an easy victory, such as Nissan is expected to have." —from C. B. H. in the San Antonio *Current* the day before the San Antonio Gran Prix (1988).

cruise-control — device for maintaining the speed of late-model American (mainly) cars on high-speed highways.

Blackie Ross and the Cruise-Control

Blackie Ross, a highliner fisherman for Basil Blades on Cape Sable Island, Nova Scotia, decided to buy a new, top of the line Cadillac, all equipped. He phoned several times to make sure it had everything: bar in the back seat, cruise-control, power windows, and so forth. Then, with Trueman Ross, his driver, he went to Motor Mart in Yarmouth to pick her up. Soon back at the fish plant, Trueman watched, horrified, as Blackie transferred into the big trunk of the new Cadillac his bait knives, rubber overalls for cutting bait, fish-scale-covered rubber boots, tool box, and a couple of haddock wrapped up in a Sobey's grocery bag. He put a 40-ouncer of rum in the bar.

Then Trueman said, "Blackie, it's hot. Let's cruise into Shelburne and get some cold beer. "

"Get aboard," said Blackie, and with Trueman proudly at the wheel, they set forth. When they had come to the 100 kph stretch of improved road beyond Barrington Head, all was going along so swimmingly that Blackie said, "Put her on automatic pilot, Trueman, and crawl into the back seat and make us some drinks!"

Now I thought that Trueman would have been the one to figure out the new automatic pilot systems on Blackie's boat. Some of the old fishermen haven't learned to manage the letters and numbers which have to be punched in to make the boat drive itself to the fishing grounds and back, turning automatically at the Groaner and Bell buoys. But it was Blackie.....

Anyhow, Trueman did as Blackie suggested. The car carried on at 110 k.p.h. straight and true for about a mile, but when they came to the bend in the highway just beyond the stinkplant, she continued ahead into the barren for about a hundred yards, fetching up at last on some rocks. The rum was broken, the car was badly damaged, and Blackie was in an ugly mood.

It would've been all right, except that Blackie insisted on suing Motor Mart for misrepresentation. He lost the case, but the accident report, a masterpiece of Canadian folk narrative, is in the files at the dealer, and it can't be copied, borrowed, or stolen.

Blackie determined to ruin that car. He left it in the swamp so long that when they came to haul her out, rats had gnawed the upholstery, trying to get at the rotting haddock in the trunk. He had it fixed, painted battleship grey, and he left it parked so many times by salt swamps, ponds, sloughs, and the ocean, that when the tow truck came to get it for the last time, the seats were sitting on the sand, the drive-shaft was sunk into the sand, and the body came away from them.

For Blackie Ross, the water is still the road.

cruiser — a marked police car. Not a **plain jane** or **weight watcher.**

cruising — Easy Riding in an automobile.

crushed Saabs — stored in a field, the old unloved, unwanted Saabs were condemned. The bill for storage hadn't been paid to the farmer who owned the land, so the car crusher, a big device on the back of an 18wheeler came on the appointed day, and the Saabs were made into little squares of metal. "Why didn't you crush that Peugeot too," the farmer asks car crusher man. "I didn't think you wanted me to," he says, "I was here for the Saabs, and that Peugeot is sorta cute."

Cunningham — race car named for its maker, Briggs Cunningham, who in 1949-1955, drove his own car, an original body design with a big American V-8 engine in the Le Mans and Sebring road races.

custom — special part designed for and fitted to your car to improve performance. See **stock.**

curber — "man who sells used car as his own." —Robert Appel, *The Used Car Believer's Handbook.*

curb surfing — usually a drunken act, colliding with a curb and surfing up onto it and perhaps onto the lawn beyond. See also **urban surfin'.**

customizing — especially in the 1950s, taking off all the trim, hood ornaments, filling in the holes with putty and carefully smoothing the surface, repainting over and over with special (metalflake) paints and waxes. The grille would be changed to a pipe grille; the bumper would be exchanged for **nerf bars**, i. e. two vertical bars (**California bumper**), **baby moon hubcaps** installed, headlights **Frenched,** and an **ooga horn** put in. For a brilliant and perceptive description of the classic customizing California car world, see Tom Wolfe's *The Kandy-Kolored Tangerine-Flake Streamline Baby* (New York: Farrar, Strauss, and Giroux, Inc., 1963).

Cutlass Supreme — rumored to be a favorite car among black customers, because the name is the same as that of the Supremes, Motown pop star group.

CVCC — on back of Hondas, means "compound vortex controlled combustion" (D. Hackett), or "controlled vortex combustion chamber", where plug ignites a small amount of rich mixture, which in turn ignites rest of chamber's lean mixture. A feature of the "new generation motor". The Japanese have performed extensive research into fuel combustion, and it shows.

C. V. T. — Continuously Variable Transmission. Expanding/contracting pulleys with belt from engine to final drive. First car, the Dutch DAF. Typical snowmobile and automatic scooter transmission. Yamahas, Hondas, etc.

C. Y. A. — another abbreviation likely from the U. S. military. Means "cover your ass," referring to the problem of estimating the price of repairs, especially for a component that is liable to malfunction repeatedly. Double, no, triple, that estimate. I personally use the "double" c. y. a. estimate factor when servicing British stuff. -j.p.

cycle / stroke — pretty technical, engineer stuff, but when you hear, as you do occasionally, "two-cycle," the distinction between "stroke" and "cycle" is being blurred. There's only one cycle in all internal combustion piston/valve engines: "suck, squeeze, bang, blow." There are two-stroke and four-stroke versions of this cycle: in the former, it goes 1) squeeze, 2) bangblowsuck; in the latter, 1) suck, 2) squeeze, 3) bang, 4) blow. Another way to distinguish the two types of engine is that on motorcycles, the ones that sound like an angry mosquito are two-strokes. The four-stroke fires once every four strokes; the two-stroke, every second stroke.

D

dab the clutch — British term: "to push quickly, not quite all the way in, just enough to change gears." A different effort is required to depress English clutch from that required for the American clutch.

daddylac — expensive car that has been given to young driver by his or her parents. —from Paul Dickson's *Slang! The Topic by Topic Dictionary of Contemporary American Lingoes.*

Daf — apparently a Russian car, referred to in Fox and Smith's masterful book of Rolls-Royce stories, but no one at Poteet Word and Motor Shop has ever seen one. Maybe now that the Berlin Wall has crumbled, we will have Dafs as well as Wartburgs to point and laugh at and admire.....

dago'd — a lowered front axle. —from Paul Burrill, Madison WI.

Daimler — persons who work at the Mercedes plant refer to it as simply "Daimler" or "Daimler-Benz". "Mercedes" isn't in their vocabulary. —Helmut Barnett, who grew up next to the Porsche factory. After World War II, he says, they built quonset type huts and made an assembly line which produced only three cars a day.

dance with who brung us — to remain completely with **stock** (factory) stuff. Chevy racers.

dashboarding it — coming to such a sudden stop that your body collides with the dashboard, knocking out teeth or worse.

dead-a-cell — parody term for the Sears Incred-a-cell battery. It is used to describe an old, used-up battery.

dead dog carpeting — installed in some, maybe most, RVs and Ford/Dodge vans. Already has spots. A concept in carpet design for restaurant and kitchen carpet. You could literally hide a dead dog on this pre-spotted carpet. Blends in with any catastrophe or stain (mustard stains, etc., are inevitable in areas where folks eat).

deader than a fart — said of a battery that shows no sign of life. Not only won't it *hold* a charge, it won't *take* a charge. This phrase has been reported in use in both Texas and Nova Scotia.

deadhead — generally means "to travel not as a customer but as an employee," as for instance when a railway conductor or airline pilot commutes to the place where work will actually commence. To **drive deadhead** was a bus term in British Columbia meaning to "return a bus to a point of origin but not picking up passengers," or "going to a bus or fire truck company and picking up and driving home the vehicle your company has purchased" and implies exceeding the speed limit.

dead man's car — a story long told in many areas is that there was a Cadillac that was for sale for a long time for $150, a late-model, all-equipped luxury car. No one would buy it, the story goes, because a person had died in it, not been found for months, and the smell could never be gotten out. The widespread range and similar details in these stories make it an urban legend, but some of them may indeed be true.

dead man throttle, switch — found on particularly dangerous machinery (like lawn mowers), consisting of a squeeze-pull clyde you have to actually have your hand on to operate the device. If one should slip and fall, say on wet grass and sloping yard, the Honda mower device, e. g. sensing that your hand is no longer on the throttle squeeze handle, disengages and brakes spinning blade to a halt, motor returns to idle. See also **impact detector.**

dead start — **bump start** with bikes not running until the drivers, waiting, gridded, get the signal and push them off, letting out the clutch and making the forward motion turn over the engines. It is important that the rider's weight put the rear wheel rubber right on the road, so that sometimes he just jumps astride the bike, like an outlaw escaping from a bank heist, waiting to straighten out his legs on each side of the seat until the bike is running, which he does classically by bracing off the handlebars with a sort of horizontal hand-stand.

dead-sticking it in — when you had borrowed your Dad's car, with the solemn promise to have it home by midnight, say, and you were very late, *and* you could see by the lights that he had probably fallen asleep, so there was an outside chance that you could shave a bit off the penalty by claiming you hadn't been all *that* late, you would cut off the engine half a block before reaching the driveway and try to coast it in. You'd say, "I had no choice but to dead-stick it in!" —from Randy, Austin (based on teen life in Houston in the days before cutting the ignition automatically locked the steering).

This term comes of course from aviation, where a "dead stick landing" was what you had to do, glide in, after engine failure.

death whine — low moan emitted by automatic transmissions just before going out. Sometimes cured/postponed by immediate fluid and filter change.

deLorean — named for the ex-GM top engineer who quit and set up a plant in New Brunswick to make it, this stainless steel car with an 80mph Renault engine and futuristic flip-up, **gull-wing** doors was rumoured to be able to last 25 years. Whatever happened to deLorean? You see the occasional deLorean car around.....in eastern Canada.

desmo — desmodromic, describing an engine which has two cam lobes for each valve, one to open the valve, one to close it, thus eliminating the valve spring or rocker arm and valve "float" at high rpm. Some Ducati motorcycles have this feature and they *scream* (from the mechanical open and closure of valves).

destruction derby — in which competitors drive into each others' old cars until only one car moves, and that one wins. Cars usually go in reverse, protecting tender radiators, using the American car's massive ass end to smash other cars. Best car for this uniquely American event, a celebration in a way of conspicuous consumption, was the 1963-64 Ford Galaxie station wagon. Also known as **demolition derby.**

detail — to vacuum the floor mats, polish the rear-view mirror, i. e. fix and make attractive anything that shows, to sell a used car without doing needed major repairs. See **Sherwin-Williams overhaul.**

detonation — mild to severe ping, usually worse when you're accelerating. Motor makes sharp metallic knocks.

deuce — a two-door car, a **coupe.** The first car so named was the 1932 Ford coupe.

deuce and a quarter — the Buick Electra 225. From Black talk, as pointed out by linguist William

Labov. Also known as a **nine** (add 'em up and you get 9).

deux chevaux — In Europe, pronounced "deuche", a short slang form, French for "two horses", a Citroen also known as the **ugly duckling.** Actually became a term for any small car; was originally a classification of small automobiles in France for taxing, licensing purposes. This car went out of production after 41 years in July of 1990. In the news story announcing its termination in Montréal's *Le Devoir* (31 March 1990) it was called "favorite of students and economy-minded travelers.....sold more than 7 million to become a symbol of folkloric France like the camembert cheese and the Basque beret.....designed as if by a driver who wanted to wear his top hat while driving.....hood made of corrugated metal....at first equipped with one headlight on the left only, because the highway code didn't at that time require two......windshield openable......fixed crank....."

Devil's Disciples — motorcycle gang in Quebec. See **Hell's Angels.**

dialed in — buzz word. Means that a machine has been finely tuned, with final settings checked by instruments.

dicing — "playing it fast and loose while competing with another driver, very much like what one has to resort to on San Antonio freeways." "Close competition with another driver." —from C. B. H. in the San Antonio *Current* the day before the San Antonio Gran Prix (1988).

dickless Tracy — a woman policeperson. Not just a cheap sexist joke: "Tracy" is a girl's name, mostly, and so the joke points up the famous cartoon detective's sexlessness. But a couple of new terms respond to the impact of this term: "Dirty Harriet syndrome" and "Jane Wayne Syndrome," both terms for women cops who are tougher than tough......

did you get any on you? — general mechanics' greeting, with unspecific or mysterious application. One such: "Yes, I did," he says, grinning, "and I scrubbed it off before I went home....and she *still* knew."

diesel — Rudolf Diesel, old German, inventor of the engine that bears his name. Without diesel engines, boat and rail and truck industries wouldn't be out of the steam engine era. Diesel fuel is

safer to store than gas, better for boats by far.
going **diesel** — knocking, suffering pre-ignition.

dieseling — said when the engine runs on for a few moments after the ignition is turned off, caused the pre-ignition from poor timing or carburetor adjustment.

digital fuel injection — fitted to lots of pseudo-new age Detroit iron. Little better than an electronic faucet for raw gasoline.

Dim Wit's Guide to Auto Repair — believe it or not, after all the condemnation of the stereotyped thinking that says women can't cope with cars, this book is listed as an item in the *New Women's Survival Guide* published by the Whole Earth Catalogue.

ding, dinged — a "ding' is a small dent in, say, a fender. "I dinged my car getting out of the parking lot again!" See also **pranged, whiskey dent.**

Upon taking possession of a new Alfa convertible, one customer pulled a small hammer from his briefcase, and in front of horrified Alfa sales people, administered a "first ding" to red shiny new fender. "Man, you are sick," white-faced **Alfisti** breathed, as though the dude had just slugged a beautiful woman right on front of him.

dingo balls — the little fuzzy balls hanging down from the fringe put up around windshield tops in **taco wagons.** —from Leonard Zwilling, staff, *Dictionary of American Regional English*.

disco volante — "flying saucer" in Italian. Prototype special model of the Alfa Spyder on which the "wing section" was very effective—front wheels took off at speed. Terrific if you like really light steering! See also **boattail, camtail, duetto.**

discredit card — a length of rubber hose for siphoning out gasoline. See also **Oklahoma credit card, New Brunswick credit card, Mexican credit card,** etc.

disc wheels — full wheel covers, instead of hubcaps. See also **moon disc, moons.**

dis machiner ist nicht fur der gerfingerpoken und rubberneck-en er mitten grabben — sign, placed on a Porsche by its American owner. When shown to a German BMW expert mechanic, Ralf Schmidt, caused same to straighten up, close one eye, and say, "I don't understand this — this isn't German!"

dispatch box — see **document box.**
distressed aluminum — where surface texture is marred (by acid, wire brush, etc.) to give aged or used (or machined) look....any look other than "stamped out," which it in fact was.

DNF — race designation, initialed beside your name on official chart, which means "did not finish." Some racers break down, others crash. A few simply head (in enduro racing) for the big tent and the cake and pie table.

doble fondo — double floor, in Spanish. Favorite "border cars" of the 1970s. "I cannot allow this vehicle to enter Mexico! ....for less than 40 dolares," the Mexican customs agent is saying, as J. D. whips out the 40, "it has a doble fondo." "Buena suerte" ("good luck"), the agent murmurs, accepting the bills.

document box — manufacturers' term, in owner's manual as late as 1953-54 Fords, for what people everywhere know as the "glove compartment." In the U. K., "glove box."

I was **dodging road turtles** — he said. Actually he was nodding off and had just about run off the dern road.

dog and pony show — an occasion when the factory reps come out and show off the new electronic and stuff such as new tools and computers.

dog car — a car that has transported dogs a lot, or has had the window left open so doggies can sleep inside. Statistically this sort of used car is worth $1100-$1700 less Blue Book value, because of dog odor, hair, scratches, etc.

doggies — cars one buys at salvage auction, as is, where is, and tows home to fix and sell with **"out-a-sight" guarantee** (guaranteed until one is out of sight, AKA **around the block guarantee.**) See also **yard dogs.**

this thing just **dogs** along at 1800-2000 rpm — said of a new Isuzu utility vehicle (small truck) with power at the low end. It is labeled "P'up" on the side, for "pickup", but people often say this means "pup." The use of dog imagery for automotive vehicles is curiously appropriate, for dogs receive from humans the same affection and contempt(when they don't work) which they give their canine pals. See **yard dogs.** To "dog" a motor", in the U. K., to "lug" it, is to try to make it work at too low an rpm.

It is also true that other animal images are used for cars: a "pig" was a term for a big mid 1960s car. (A Quebecois term for such a car was **minoune,** a fat female cat). One Nova Scotian who was defensively bragging about the pickup he caused to throw a rod while racing on a country road said "It always was a hot animal, anyway."

Volkswagen made a successful use of this habit by nicknaming its little car the "beetle." Plymouth made a "barracuda."

doghouse — the engine cover on Ford and Dodge vans. Made of fiberglass, the size and shape explains the name. And, in a pinch, you could make a fine sizable doghouse out of an old one.

dogtracking — going down the road like a hound dog runs, with rear end off to the side a little (or a lot, depending. Indicative of bent or twisted frame.)

Do It Right the First Time — Sign in local Austin Toyota dealership. Actually means "You will do it right....no matter if it takes you more than once." A shop with good morale has, always, a cameraderie which doesn't permit a neophyte mechanic to flounder around a problem very long. They help him get to the root of the problem. After all, they might learn something new. [Ed.: new and interesting ways of breaking down are always coming in.] Mass-produced cars by their mass-produced nature share their weaknesses and thus predictable ways. If one has a weak part, all of them have it.

domestic sports car — seriously, folks, there ain't no such thing. The Corvette and the 1956 T-bird ain't sports cars. The 'Vette, with its big V-8, has deadly understeer, and the rear end squirrels around like it had oil on the tires all the time. The T-bird, with its 427 (425 hp) could go like its tail was on fire in a straight line (and only in a straight line). They aren't raced much. For a dissenting opinion, see John Lawlor's list under **sports car.**

donorcycle rider — motorcycle rider without helmet. From medical talk (emergency room personnel).

he **don't mind dyin'** — said in admiration and awe of a particularly daring wild man motorcycle racer as he slide-drifted an amazing corner.

Don't OverDo, Go Easy — what else? D O D G E!

Don't worry, be happy driving philosophy — From 60s guru of happiness Meher Baba, whose smiling face adorned the dashboards of countless VW buses and other hip driving machines. I assume that all of these believers are long gone now, some recanted, some mowed down from behind by big trucks, etc.

dooley — pickup truck with four wheels (two axles) in rear, used for pulling gooseneck trailers. "Dooley" is derived from "dual," but **duals** are twin exhaust pipes, not wheels and tires.

doolies, dualies — dual exhaust pipes.

doomaflockie — name for any object you can't remember the right name for. Also known as a **clyde, thingamajigger, chingaso, chingadera.**

Do or Don't Go Ever — derogatory explanation of the name Dodge.

doorhandle it — cornering at the limit, as in "I was doorhandling it up my favourite backroad." Also called **cornering on the doorhandles**, or leaning a car over so far the doorhandles are about to scrape on the pavement. Similar to footpeg grinding on a motorcycle (racers sometimes discover after a gruelling race that the footpegs are actually sharpened!)

doorslammer — from drag racing, a type of car which actually still has doors that open and close, as distinguished from cars you have to get into through the top, by climbing through the window, etc.

doozy, Dusie, *Duesy* — originally, the Duesenberg, an old, classic, long, low, very gaudy car. A January 1989 survey of "the ten best performance cars" by Csaba Csere in *Car and Driver* lists the 1934 Duesenberg SJ as "a model of hedonistic refinement" and at the time "the world's highest-performance street car." Hence the (now fairly extinct itself) expression meaning anything fairly impressive, overdone, e. g. a hangover.

double bubble — the Italian bodybuilder Zagato built many aerodynamic coupe bodies on various Italian chassis; the bodies were so low that often the roof had a pair of bumps in it for clearance for the driver's and passenger's heads; this type of body became known as a "double bubble."

double-clutching — the proper way to shift old truck gearboxes. The only way to shift the 31 M type MG. In U. K. known as "double de-clutching." A British car fan comments: "sorry, we *change* gear in U. K., and not because we're 'shiftless.'"

double knocker — a double overhead camshaft engine.

double pumper — a four-barrel carburetor. According to Tom Brown, "a four barrel Holley carb with all four barrels set up as primaries; the name comes from the fact that each pair of barrels had its own accelerator pump and float bowl."

double wide, triple ugly — said of motor homes.

doughnut — a **burn out** made in the shape of a circle. "That young fool did another doughnut in my yard last night!"
— the tiny spare tire provided with rental cars.

down, down time — undergoing repairs. Also known as "time in prison." "It'll be down for about a week for that overhaul". Jaguars used to be the king here, partly due to unavailability of parts and frequent breakdowns. The change to Bosch fuel injection improved their record a lot. Alfa Romeo was another highliner in this area.

down to the rivets — said of worn out brake pads or clutch.

draft — "not beer but the 'hole' left in the air by a car at high speed. A following car can use the suction to get a bit of a free ride, and use less power. You can do the same thing behind a big truck on the highway, but it's not really a good idea." —from C. B. H. in the San Antonio *Current* the day before the San Antonio Gran Prix (1988). "Drafting" is extremely important in bicycle racing; if a pack of bicycle racers coordinate their speed and configuration, taking turns taking the lead, they all go faster. Known also as **slipstreaming.**

drag coefficient — a number....the lower the better, indicating how "slippery" a car's shape is to wind drag (for example, old VW microbus would have a relatively high Cd or properly Cx (.4 or .5), whereas a Porsche 911 or Lamborghini would be low (.3). A mid or late 70s Cadillac Eldorado would be in the low .5s. Anything in the low .3s is good; anything in the .4s is not so good. The faster you go, the more air you push, and the more horsepower you need; thus above 70 or 80 mph, the drag coefficient, the "aerodynamic loss," becomes significant, actually increases power required to propel the car along. An engineer's way to write "drag" is "$^{1/2PV}{}_{2}Scd$", i. e. varies as square of speed. 90mph = 9 times force at 30.

drag gas — leaded, very high octane premium gasoline (100- 105 octane, where premium normally is around 93 octane).

draw — to a mechanic, "the draw" is the amount of amperage a starter draws from the battery to spin the motor over. Excessive draw means a worn starter motor.

dresser, dressed up, full dress, full dresser — car with fender skirts, fur on dash, plastic Jesus or St. Christopher (or both) on dash. "Dresser" is also short for "full dress Hog," a Harley 74 with complete rig—saddlebags, extra taillights, radio, etc. Any tour bike (Honda, Kawa, Suzuki, Yamaha, can be dressed up.

drift — the action of centrifugal force on the tires of a car in a curve.

Drive — one of several "smart car" systems to give navigation and control assistance to help move traffic through congested areas. "Dedicated Road Infrastructure for Vehicle Safety in Europe": "In phase one (1988-1001), $170-million was put into developing technology for smart highway systems, including access controls to freeways, urban traffic management, and in-car route selection. In phase two, $240-million is being spent on evaluation." —Timothy Pritchard, "Smart Cars down the road," Toronto *Globe and Mail,* February 1, 1993. See also **Prometheus, Pathfinder, TravTek.**

drive by wire — a new car feature on the 1988 BMW 750i V-12. There is no throttle cable. The footpedal gives an electrical command to the computer. The computer gives the command to the throttle linkage under the hood, and the engine accelerates or decelerates. "Don't like the sound of it," my welder says. "What if the computer goes **haywire**?" From aircraft talk, where it was "fly by wire." The F-16 is totally "fly by wire," and the Concorde was the first commercial plane to do so. The computer is programmed so that fatal maneuvers cannot be done by manual override, "the ape can't kill himself". What must be avoided is loss of control resulting from "G-lock", "G-force induced loss of consciousness."

The Rover had this feature, "drive by wire," on a road test version in the late 1950s.

.**driveway rocket** — an Audi 5000 automatic acquired this irreverent name as the result of some accidents which led to well-publicized court cases. The company was acquitted, and informed but objective engineering people tend to blame the loose nut behind the wheel, but the company changed the name of the model and the placement of the foot pedals..... See **unintended acceleration.**

driving dark — police term for following someone with lights out at night, to determine if they are DWI, etc.

dropped — lowered, "sometimes a whole car, one end, or a headlight bar." —from Paul Burrill, Madison WI.

dropped valve — usually catastrophic. When valve stem breaks and lets valve face fall into the works, **lunching** the piston, other valves. Air cooled VWs do this. See also **swallow a valve.**

drunk bumps — see **city titties.** See also **rumble strips, zip strips, wake bumps.**

the **drunk's distance** — "Give that one the drunk's distance." (Distance your car several car lengths from a driver obviously drunk!) In all prudence, drivers who are dizzy or confused for any reason (fatigue, having had **one** too many **for the road**) should keep this extra precautionary distance from all other traffic, too.

dry sump — racing modification. Oil is pumped out of the oil pan faster than the lubrication system pumps it in, via the crank and cam and valve gear, thus allowing crankshaft to achieve higher rpm, more power, because the crankshaft is "dragging" through the oil. Originally developed for airplanes, because with the engine sometimes flying upsidedown, etc., you couldn't rely on the reservoir of oil to flow out by gravity. For other automobile terms and bits of technology derived from the airplane, see also **Dzus fasteners, supercharging,** and think "fly low."

duals, dual exhausts — twin, doubled, exhaust systems with mufflers and exhaust pipes specially installed to give higher performance. A **bad boy car** standard modification.

duck lights — the dim lights on a car, Nebraska, 1960s, according to the *Dictionary of American Re-*

gional English. See also **city lights.**

duetto — Original Alfa Spyder convertible, for its twin 2-barrelled Weber carburetors, and resultant beautiful sound of the pipes. See also **disco volante, boattail, camtail.**

Dukes of Hazzard — Those dudes on TV, always jumping that Dodge over stuff, and driving away in a cloud of dust .... are actually *destroying the suspension* almost every time they fly through the air and land on the other side of the creek. They have 25 of those fast Dodges, all of them in the frame shop daily on a rotating basis.

D.U.K.W. — Army "duck",. amphibious truck/vessel. Huge, ugly, more at home in the water than on land.

dummy — anyone who doesn't wear seat belts. Also, mannequin used to study impact of car crashes on human body.

dumping the clutch — letting out on the clutch pedal abruptly, causing the car to **burn off** or **bark the tires.** Also called **popping the clutch.**

dumps — illegal if cable operated from driver's seat, dumps are dual side pipes in addition to regular exhaust system, which are blocked, and usually heavily chromed. The end plates blocking the dump pipes have to be bolted shut, by state law. In the 1950s and early 60s cable operated dumps added a real big flash and roar to yer V-8, as you blew flames (literally) out to the side with each shift of gears. Bad boy stuff like this only exists in little town in California and the Texas border, where the Feds and the Environmental Protection Agency haven't scared local inspection stations. It's illegal to mess with your modern car's catalytic exhaust system.

D W I, D U I — "driving while intoxicated," "driving under the influence", "driving while impaired." See **502.**

Dzus fasteners — a sort of clip, using a flush-fitted key-turnable latch, for, e. g. hood and fender skirts. Designed for minimum wind resistance, and first developed for airplanes.

E

Eagle — Dan Gurney's racing team/cars....American built and very successful racing cars (open-wheeled Formula I and GT class).

easing him into the wall — "a bit of racing fun and games frowned upon by officials." "First made popular in 'Ben Hur'."—from C. H. B. in the San Antonio *Current* the day before the San Antonio Gran Prix (1988).

easy rider — lying back, smoking up, and driving fast. Think Peter Fonda. A kind of motorcycle, too, with high handlebars, back-slanted seat, **ape-hangers**?

eat its lunch — jocular way to say that an engine has suffered total and terminal failure. See also **go south on you, go west on you.** This expression may have been adapted from lawyers' talk, or more likely, contributed to it: in an essay on freedom of the press legislation in the September 1989 Harper's titled "The Quiet Coup," by Philip Weiss, a prosecutor says, "'I would have eaten his lunch,' Schatzow said when I asked him why Morison didn't testify." The context suggests "I would have eaten *him* for lunch."

eat the dash — emergency medical team word for what happens in even relatively mild collisions to people's faces who aren't buckled up.

econobox — Suzuki Swift and other such.....1900 lbs., 170 hp., 3 cyls., 1300 cc.

economy mode — as opposed to **sport mode**, one of two settings for the steering and suspension damper (i. e. on or off) made necessary in the Mazda RX-7 by the rotary engine, which in hard acceleration, has a twisting torque effect on the whole little whiz-box! See also **Porsche baiter.**

Edsel — a model of Ford introduced, then discontinued, during the late 1950s. Its name became synonymous, perhaps unjustifiably, with **lemon.** ("An Oldsmobile sucking on a lemon" was one well-known description of the body style. The lemon referred to the distinctive "horse-collar" design in the middle of the front grille). Named for Henry Ford's son. Every Day Something Else Louses up? Statistics reveal that only one

Edsel has been stolen, and that was in the dark ("I thought it was a Ford or something.")

E. G. R. — see **pollution control devices.**

Egyptian brake pedal — the horn, according to P. J. O'Rourke, in *Holidays in Hell* (Vintage, 1989), p. 71. He points out that in Egypt, as in all third-world countries, drivers routinely honk 1) when anything blocks the road, 2) when anything doesn't block the road, 3) when anything *might* block the road, 4) at red lights, 5) at green lights, and 6) at all other times.

not hitting on all **eight** — said of a person who is acting as if he is mentally deficient or disabled. The eight refers, obviously, to eight cylinders, as in "not firing on all eight cylinders". See also **one wheel in the sand** or **snow.** Other variants are "one brick shy of a load," "not playing with a full deck."

einspritzer — source of the "e" in old model names of Mercedes, for the name of the device that is the key to fuel injection. See **spritzer.**

elephant snot — mechanics' term for Permatex coppercoat gasket seal. See also **gorilla snot.**

Engine Management System — "usually found on the GTP cars, it is an on board computer which monitors the engine's performance and keeps it running at top efficiency."

endo — to go end over end, "pitchpole." Motorcycles do it. Sprint cars do it. And it is possible to flip a car end over end going over jumps, **whoops**, etc. This is a sort of ballistic maneuver which no one short of Evel Knievel has performed intentionally. Usually done after or near a ramp or jump in a racetrack, accompanied by lots of crashing and breaking and tinkling sounds, not to mention human pain and suffering. Remember to back off on the throttle just as you enter the jump. —*Motocross Cat.*

Engineer's blue — British term for "Prussian blue." Not a car paint color, the term refers to special blue paint used to paint parts which need to be scribed, or marked. Since you can't see marks on metal, the paint is applied, then a line is made in the paint. Also used for "scraping in" white metal bearing shell locations at big ends of connecting rods on crankshaft. "Dad spent a week doing this during what was supposed to be a vacation when the big ends went on our old car on the first day out."

Enzo Ferrari — Italian automaker, of beautiful, fast V-12s, the cars of kings and rock stars. It was his son Dino Ferrari for whom the V-8 "Dino" Ferrari was named. Enzo was 1930s Alfa race team manager, during the days when the Alfa team was battling the Germans, Mercedes and Auto-Union, which were funded massively by Adolf Hitler.

error code — how modern cars are "trouble shot": the mechanic plugs "black box" into car's electrical system, pushes buttons, and out comes error code, telling him what happened (event) and what burned out.

Estate car, Estate waggon — British terms for "station wagon."

ethyl — old fashioned high octane leaded premium gasoline, no longer available. See also **drag gas.**

event — modern day computer word for malfunction, and all concurrent stuff (fire, smoke, etc.) I. e.: Well, the 'event' musta happened when you went over a bump and your battery slipped its holddown and shorted and burned the wiring harness out."

Exspectrum — derogatory nickname for Chevy's Spectrum.

expensive noise — "It made a very expensive noise and then stopped completely!" — spoken by a member of Parliament, I believe, of his Jaguar.

Charges to Fix

Ping ping ping	$20
Ping thud ping	$30
Ping Clank Thud	$40
Clank thud bonk	$70
Clank Bang clank	$400
Bang Bang Bang	$1000

let's see it **exploded** — what the auto parts man sees in his book, an engineers' technical drawing showing the engine parts displayed separately in order of their working place. As if exploded.

eye in the sky — police helicopter. this one has **eyes** — he says, sliding the starter into place. "Eyes" are a feature of a piece that fits well and goes into place easily.

F

factory tint — an option offered to the original buyer, not added in later **custom** work, like "E-Z Eye glass." Another option is, for example, **factory air** (air conditioning).

fag cars — car talk term for automobiles in fashion with the male gay community. E. g. old DeSotos.

fallen rider pass — passing, using the fallen rider to advantage. Some else has to avoid a fallen rider, and gets passed as a result.

if it **falls out** — "I dunno," the mechanic said, peering up through the fender well at the well hidden starter. "If it falls out, which it ain't gonna, it'd be 20 bucks or so labor, and $69.50 for the rebuilt starter....I think it'll take longer than an hour to get it in and out, and that's forty dollars an hour labor."

If it falls out.... expression of amount of work involved in removing and replacing a component. (Sports cars and, hell, lots of modern cars, are real crowded under the hood. Besides the basics, layers of emission controls, vacuum thingamajigs, hoses, etc., clutter up the engine compartments. Mechanics often make **road maps** — mental or physical drawings — of the stuff they unhook and take off to get to a component.)

Fastback — sedanette with torpedo shape—flattened-out rear end.

fast chip — these new computer controlled ignition-fuel injection cars are controlled—believe it or not—by a chip. And some say you can get "fast" chips which deliver more stuff, earlier, to those power-crazed cylinders.

Fat Bob Harley — a Harley-Davidson motorcycle with two separate gas tanks bolted on each side. Referred to in Hunter Thompson's *Songs of the Doomed*, p. 280.

father-son switch — a device sometimes put on a really hot car, one with three two-barrel carburetors on a six-cylinder engine, e. g. (see **three deuces**), in order for the father to cut out two of the carburetors so as to reduce the power, which in turn would reduce the chances that the son would abuse the car when he was off driving it by drag-racing it on the highway, taking curves too fast, etc.

when the **fat lady is singing** — the sound your automatic transmission/power-steering unit/air conditioning compressor, etc., makes when it is self destructing and it's all over. "It's not over until the fat lady sings," in cars, as in opera.

fat tires — "they pick up every nail in the road, so *we* won't get flat tires."

fault finding — customary British term for "troubleshooting."

fender bender — rhyming slang for a minor accident. See **ding, pranged, whiskey dent, smished.**

fender skirts — accessory body item popular in the 1950s, a clamp-on metal cover for the wheel-well opening.

Ferrari — see **Enzo Ferrari.**

Ferry Porsche — son of Dr. Ferdinand Porsche, torchbearer of the Porsche banner and member of the German parliament.

Fiasco — Ford Fiesta. German Ford **beercan** car.

FIAT — acronym: "Fix it Again, Tony." Born **F**abrication **I**taliani **A**utomobili **T**urino. A BMW mechanic from Germany reports scornfully that sometimes the *new* Fiats won't start as they are about to be driven onto the delivery trailer for transport to the dealers, but have to be towed or winched aboard.
"How many Italians fit into a Fiat?" "Poppa, Momma, brother, sister, grandma, grandpa, and the dog."

"Fuel pump for a Fiat?" he says. "Lessee here......we've probably got some flat ones around here somewheres." Fiat makes wordleap to Flat, possibly because of what would happen in a truck-Fiat collision).

Fiera — name of a model of Pontiac in 1984 which means "very proud" in Italian. Not to be confused with Ciera, or Fiesta. Or Sierra. "Fiera" means "ugly old woman" in Spanish. What's with these "ia" words in a proud American domestic industry? As Cecil Adams (*Straight Dope*) says, "No wonder the Japanese are killing us!" See **Pinto.**

fifth dimension — a place where dropped and lost small nuts and bolts go. "I can't find it — it must have gone into the fifth dimension."

film strength — tendency of a substance to stick to a surface.

Next time you "Armor-All" your dashboard, just get some on the windshield and try to scrub it off. Armor-All and other silicones, used as protectants from sunlight, should be sprayed on a cloth and wiped onto surfaces which are next to glass.

fine tuner — sledge hammer. See also **inertia wrench, whop stick.**

put it through **finishing school** — to fix all of the little things on a customer's list, as distinguished from major problems. That is, to deal with such problems as window and door squeaks, loose nuts and bolts, mirrors, etc. Called **sweetening** at the Rolls-Royce factory: "Engineers spend up to four days 'sweetening' (i. e. removing the tiniest flaw) the bare body shell of a Rolls-Royce before the 14-stage painting process begins." —Fox and Smith, *Rolls-Royce: The Complete Works.*

firecracker — lights on top of a cop car. See also **gumball machine, cherry.**

firewalling it — same as "one foot in the carburetor," driving so fast that you run right against the firewall. Or, in the cockpit, (likely originated in aviation), pushing the throttle to the firewall.

first — being the first to the corner, taking everyone off the start.... Certainly makes the cornering easier (cornering in the middle of the pack is like roller-skating in a buffalo herd, go down and you're dog meat).

fish — Citroen (French car): "looks like a ......" The name of this car, unintentionally funny to speakers of English, echoes the French word for "lemon", "citron."

fish bait — old wornout V-8 motor sunk into lake. Hence any wornout piece of automotive scrap.

fishheads — jocular term for Japanese cars. See also **sushimobiles, rice burners.** Not much used since their reliability has become clear.

fishing weight — any carburetor with a bad reputation, e. g. the Solex two-barrel on old German cars.

fishtail — to cause the rear end of the car to spin around or go from side to side by breaking the rear wheels loose, either by pulling on the emergency brake and twisting the wheel at a bit of speed, on a gravel road, or goosing a rear-wheel drive car and playing the wheel from left to right and back again. An enthusiastic experiment indulged by new drivers. See also **Lazy J, doughnut.**

502 — the California term for **DWI, DUI.**

five window coupe — "a two-door, two passenger car with little windows in the side behind the door windows. All but the windshield are counted." —from Paul Burrill, Madison WI. See also **three-window coupe.**

did you **fix it? No, I J B Welded it!** — J. B. Weld is a superglue, but still.....

fix the air leaks — the only legal reason for unplugging the emission control equipment, a modification popular with drivers who like high performance. "I had to do it: I was fixing the air leaks!"

Fix or Repair Daily — derogatory explanation of the imaginary acronym formed by the word FORD. Others are **Fucked Over Rebuilt Dodge, Found on the Road Dead, Frequent overheating, rapid depreciation, Fucken Old Rebuilt Datsun.** Ford owners say it means **First on Race Day** (only American car Le Mans winner! in the mid-1960s)

Driving by the Ford factory in Germany, I ask Ralf if European fords are any better than American ones. He smiles, "Ford is Ford, the world over." "You mean, smoking, knocking, overheating?" I ask, "like the American Fords?" He nods, and we both laugh.

flags at the race track —

green flag - race is under way the instant it is displayed (chief starter's flag)

yellow flag - motionless = caution. Waved = danger. No passing on yellow flags.

yellow and red striped flag - oil has been spilled on the track.

white flag - ambulance is on course.

blue flag - steady = you're being followed

blue flag - waved = he wants to pass

senna - he's going to try (Formula 1)

blue and yellow striped flag - someone is following you close. Let him pass.

red flag - stop the race.

black flag - complete the lap you are now on, then pull into pit.

black flag with word "all" displayed on blackboard - race stopped, complete lap you are now on and pull into pit.

furled black flag - warning: you are driving in an unsafe manner and if you continue you will be blackflagged.

(*meatball* flag) - black flag with orange ball in center - there is something mechanically wrong with your vehicle. Get off course and get outta town.

checkered flag - you have finished the race (or practice).

Budweiser flag, Labatt flag, etc.- you are in proximity of beer.

Presidential flag - you are in proximity of the presidential limo. Drive slow, be polite, hide the beer.

flame job — special paint job for hot rods, especially in the 50s, which decorated it with flames appearing to come out of the engine compartment, along the sides of the hood and front doors.

flameout — from aviation jets, to totally lose power, have engine shut down, etc.

flames — painted flames on fenders almost went out in the 50s, but now are back. **Low riders** have flames.

flame throwers — "exhaust tips with spark plugs mounted on them. A rich gas mixture is run into the pipe, a magneto fires the spark plug, and a flame shoots out the exhaust tip." —from Paul Burrill, Madison WI.

flangegasket — said as one word, usually between mechanics. Means "fantastic." "Well, if you can have it ready by noon, that'd be just flangegasket, Leroy."

flat, flat out — expert, top performance, fast driving. "How a driver always describes his performance on the curves to the team manager, no matter what the reality. Or, it can mean a 'tired,' worn out engine, an engine which has gone 'off song.'"

flathead — earliest Harley-Davidson, Indian motorcycles also (God made 'em that way, son). See also **knuckle head, shovel head, pan head, block head.**

flatheads rule — proverb of the 1950s. Old Ford V-8s were kings of the dragstrip because Ford had the first production V-8s (since 1932) when Chevys still only had the **hot water 6,** also known as the **stovebolt six**.

flat-spotting — condition which causes a thumping noise on the highway at speed just after a car is driven first when it has been sitting a long time. Nylon cords tended to develop flat spots. See **nylon thump**.

flavor — model, type, size, of, say, brake pad. "What flavor do you want," says the parts man, "We got organics, semi-metallics, metallics, original equipment." "What flavor of BMW are we talking about," I ask the customer. "It's a 535i," he says. It's a word for model, type, size, as if you were standing there talking to the ice cream man.

flip-flop — among experts on car fancy painting, a "black cherry flip-flop" is a colour that changes under different light conditions.

flivver — a really old term, probably not much in use since the 'thirties, for an old car. "Fliv" was "to fail or flop." —*Dictionary of American Slang*.

float the valves — to **over-rev** an engine, racing it so fast that the valves (especially hydraulic ones) can't close. It can blow the motor. The point of hydraulic valve lifters was that they cushioned shock, but only up to a certain speed. For an analogous disaster, see **swallow a valve.**

Floating the valves was defeated by Ducati with something called a "desmodromic valve." Complete description available by applying in person at Poteet Motors with a six-pack of cold beer.

flog — adapted from Western cowboy talk? — "to drive the hell out of...."....."drive the living shit out of," ...."to drive the holy living shit out of.....", "to drive the dog shit out of......."

floorboard — in almost all cars anyone now alive knows, the "floor" of the car is made of metal. It was not always so. The story goes that Henry Ford, for the Model-T, had parts made in various places and shipped to his assembly plant, but he specified exactly what crates the parts were to be shipped in, right down to the type of wood, where the knotholes could be, etc. When one shipment arrived, the guards refused it, not on the grounds that the parts were defective, but because the crates weren't up to specifications. When the guards at the plant were asked about this, they said, "We use the crates to make the floorboards on the Model-T!"

floorboard it — accelerate. Also known as **floor it, hotfoot it, nail it, stand on it, launch time, peel rubber.**

fluid coupling — the key, among other things, to automatic transmissions. The power comes from one end and drives a turbine structure which propels the fluid, which in turn, when driven hard enough, propels another turbine to transmit power onward, say, to the wheels. The solid parts never touch, and when the speed is reduced, the torque is disconnected.

flush-o-matic — automatic transmission installed in and sometimes rejected by American Motors cars (e. g. Ramblers).

flutter valve — an obsolete part from the Hupmobile, now remembered by mechanics in joking. It was a small piece of metal held in place by a weak spring, opened by atmospheric pressure under suction.

Another one was on a monster, O. B. O'Malloy's Kruger-Atlas **make-and-break** engine, manufactured in San Antonio Texas in 1915; big as a car and spinning two 5-foot diameter flywheels, it chuffed about three times per minute, going into a freewheel cycle with exhaust valve held open thus de-activating intake flutter valve between chuffs. Once rpms dropped, governor mechanism closed exhaust valve, and ka-chuff, it sped the flywheels up to 250 rpm, shaking the ground and the air with each chuff.

flying brick — slang term, a deliberate slur, applied by **Boxer Twin** riders to the new "K" BMW motorcycle, so nicknamed because of the square engine, which looks like a big aluminum brick going down the road with wheels attached to it at either end. The "K" is asymmetrical, as the bulk of the square engine sticks out to one side only, unlike the Boxer Twin.

following too close — "Those people behind us are too close," I say to almost asleep brother Dewey.

"Simple," he murmurs, still almost asleep. "Move over in the lane a little bit and spray them with gravel. I move over. It works. White crushed granite, courtesy of the Texas Highway Department, sprays the front of their car like crazy. They were eyeballing our dirt bikes. They fade back fast, swerving wildly to avoid the machine-gun-like blast. I wave and try to look it was an accident.

foot nailed to the juice — driving the car as fast as it can go. Pedal to the metal. **WFO.** —from Jim Dodge's *Not Fade Away*.

footprints on the ceiling — literal and figurative expression for a well used car that shows wear and tear from kids, dogs, etc.

forty-five mph warning light — Greg's father's pride and joy, a 1945 MG TD, has among other things an amber light on the dash which comes on and warns you when you reach or exceed 45 mph. Who sez time travel is impossible: drive it and drift away.

Ford — First on Race Day. To others, "Fix or Repair Daily." "In Ford Country, on a quiet night, you can hear a Ford rust."

Formula Racing — International, rules by FSA, Federation Internationale Sportive Automobile. Minimum weight, engine size, etc. F1 and FIII current—whatever happened to F2?

Formula III — unusual auto racing class developed in England after World War II, in which 500cc twin-cylinder motorcycle rear engines powered little 300 lb. cars bodied from aircraft drop tanks, using a chain drive to the differential. Stirling Moss drove in this class.

Found on Road Dead — F O R D (especially as in Pinto) —Tom Brown.

four-wheel drift — in car racing, a controlled slide, sliding all four wheels instead of just the rear wheels, going fast on a curve so close to the technically possible index "where the rubber meets the road," that the driver may be said to **break it loose.**

four-wheelers — one of the latest evolutionary strains (angel or beast?) in the motorcycle, the ATV (All-Terrain Vehicle) is interesting in that for a brief period there have been motorcycles that had more wheels than certain cars (see **three-wheelers)** Don Hackett has suggested that the ultimate question to ask in classifying a vehicle as a motorcycle or car is "do you sit in it or on it?" But even this test may not cover all: there are superexpensive, superelaborate motorcycles with fairings that provide shade, shelter, and a show—whether they provide safety as well is a real question.

four on the floor — 4-speed manual transmission, so named because originally the gearshift lever was on the floorboard, rather than the steering column. But the full story is that actually after it was on the floorboard it spent years on the steering column, and the return to the floorboard was slow and rare, and **four on the floor** got its name during this return, associated with "sports machinery."

four wheel drive — the true use of four-wheel drive, Michael says, "putting it into 4-wheel when the theatre parking lot is clogged....cars waiting to get out, back out, anything, no one moving, engines all running, hundreds of cars going nowhere." He drives over the concrete pillar in front of the parking grass, crushing a small shrub in the lawn of the office building. "I know these lawyers in this building," he says, driving across their lawn, creating two huge ruts in the soft mushy lawn. Banging over the curb, Michael gains the street, and traffic parts to let the big lurching truck enter.......

frag — to fragment an engine, blow it so completely that pieces of motor come through the side of the engine block, lots of smoke, etc.

frammis — a term used to describe a part which a customer probably cannot know about or understand, and doesn't need to. Like a **thingamajig, clyde, dingus,** etc. Probably from "diaphragm."

Frenched headlights — no ring around the headlight, body built out to enclose the light itself. A feature of car customizing which also appears, in modified form, on the 1980s Rolls Royce Silver Shadow II.

frog — this one is a yellow Ford tractor. The Ford letters in its grille were moved thusly — O and R reversed, D letter taken off and sawed in pieces and glued back together to make a G......

frog car — term for any French car—Peugeot, Renault, Citroen. Also known as **yogurt makers.**

fry test — also known as the "sizzle test". When plugging in a substitute fuel pump relay or other non-authorized electrical parts substitution, when you have to turn it on, energize the system; this is the "fry test." If it flies, go with it; if it fries, turn it off and repair the wiring harness.

F U B A R — **f**ucked **u**p **b**eyond **a**ll **r**ecognition. Said of a part or bolt that is so badly damaged that you can't even tell what it was, or what it was for. A term from WWII Navy, a relative of SNAFUed.

Fuego — Who in their right mind (Mexican taxi operators excluded) would own a car named "fire"? (I saw three Latin types pushing one down Lamar Boulevard in Austin tonight).

fueler, fuel dragster — burns **nitromethane**. A **nitro rig.**

fuelie — 1957 car slang for then-optional fuel injection (available on Bel-Air and Corvette). Also available were two 4-barrel carburetors with 270 BHP.

F. U. J. M. O — Fuck you, Jack, move over. Stencilled in large letters on back of Camaros, etc. seen on the Houston freeway. For years now it has been almost literally *war* to drive on Houston's crowded, anarchic freeways —hot, humid, overtaxed systems, and most definitely unfriendly.....

full bore — in its most common use, means "pedal to the metal," **WFO**, accelerating as much as possible. Derived from "boring out" the cylinders, to put in oversize pistons and increase power and performance. See also **foot nailed to the juice.**

full Cleveland — used car salesman wearing white tie, white belt, white shoes, plaid jacket. —from Click and Clack Brothers, National Public Radio's Car Talk show. In Anne Soukhanov's "Word Watch" column in the August1992 *Atlantic* there is a discussion (with some followup letters in the November issue) of this phrase which refers to its wider use as a description of a flashy style of dressing; thus the application to used car salesmen may be a derivation of an earlier use. See also **checkered sports coat award.** We have also found informants who recall the use of this phrase, full Cleveland, to refer to certain Fords that had engines built totally in Cleveland, rather than only of parts some of which were made in Cleveland and others in Detroit; they were reputedly more reliable, more powerful, etc.

full house mouse — "small car that's been modified for higher performance," according to John Lawlor's *How to talk car*. "A souped VW, for example, is a full house mouse."

full moon — to show one's ass to a car being passed, with window rolled down. If testicles are displayed, it's a **full moon with loose tools.** See also **pressed ham, half moon.**

fun factor — other way of saying "my power to weight ratio." I. e. a 948 cc. Austin Healy Sprite weighing about 1200 pounds is as much fun to drive as an overpowered Corvette. See **corkscrew.**

funny car — a class of drag racer. Has to have a CAR BODY, as opposed to a pure dragster such as a **rail job, slingshot,** etc. A true dragster is not a stock car by any stretch of the imagination, can be easily **blown,** etc.

furious — a very small engine that has to turn a whole lot of **revs** to compete for the road. I. e. the two-cylinder Honda 600 car.

G

galled — as in "galled camshaft," where surface is marred by friction, lack of oil, etc.

garage cat — a cat comfortable enough around cars and car repair shops that it doesn't mind getting grease on its back.

Garfield ordinance — a way to describe a town with a wrecked or dead car in every yard. "They have the Garfield ordinance in force: if you don't have one in your yard, they'll bring one over and it'll break down!" Named for Garfield, Texas, a classic of its kind.

gardening — from flat track racing, like a "burnout" in dirt, having to do with the arrangement of your place in the starting line dirt. Some riders dig little exit **berms** and others dig a trench, hoping to psych out the other starters. I saw Heikki Mikkola, the Flying Finn, do a series of third gear-leaning over the bars-full-throttle, semi-wheelie starts.....and it would have thoroughly psyched me to be near him on a machine....he went so fast off the starting line his roostertail covered everyone into the first turn.

gasahol, gasohol — gasoline with up to 10% methanol. Sold in California first, and then all over the 'States. In a summer, 1988 article in *Rural Delivery*, a farm journal published in Port Joli, Nova Scotia, Rance Spitler points out that because alcohol combines much more readily with water than does gasoline, these gas-alcohol mixes can destroy a chainsaw or indeed any two-stroke engine.

gas-guzzler — a car which because of great weight, many cylinders, and/or inefficient tuning uses a lot of gasoline in order to operate. This term, as more and more cars are using fuel injection rather than a carburetor (to mix air and gas) is becoming obsolete. Also known as **gas-hog.**

gasoline — smell of. Always investigate. Gasoline can explode with great energy. Unless you just filled up with gas and spilled a little of it, the smell of gas is trouble. Under the hood gas leaks cause engine fires.

gawk factor — cop term for what happens when a traffic jam forms up and folks drive slowly by the four-car pileup, gawking at the gnarly wreckage.

gear drive — "driving the camshaft by gears instead of chain. Causes a distinctive sound." —from Paul Burrill, Madison WI.

gear flogger — truck driver.

gear heads — "ardent race fans." —from CHB.

gearshift — this ordinary, well-known name of the control lever in every motor vehicle takes on added lustre in an adapted use by a member of the Crickets, Buddy Holly's rockabilly backup band in the 1950s: "Buddy Holly always bought the best of anything. He brought the first Fender Stratocaster into Lubbock. It was the first solid-body guitar I'd ever seen; it had a **gearshift** on it!" — laugh — from The Buddy Holly Story, documentary film.

Generous Motors — ironic term applied to his employer by a U. S. GM employee during a protracted labor struggle.

gerbil around — verb. To climb around, under, on a car, to look busy without getting a whole lot done. Usually used to describe novice mechanics' attempts to diagnose a problem by trying out this or that test in no particular order, usually unsuccessfully.

German chrome — silver spray paint.

to go down like a **German fighter plane** — trailing lots of smoke. Lots of German cars do this too....VWs, Porsches, BMWs.

get a bigger hammer — traditionally, a Chevrolet mechanic's ultimate rule of thumb. Does not work on British machines.

get a ride — be sponsored, i .e. get a race car to drive in a race.

ghost car — an **unmarked** police car, possibly but not necessarily a **weight watcher. Plain jane.**

gilligan hitch — "any method of binding with a chain." —from the *Dictionary of American Regional English*, citing Ken Weaver's *Texas Crude.*

Gimli glider — "the Gimli glider was the Air Canada aircraft that ran out of fuel on a flight from the East to Edmonton on July 23, 1983, and glided to a landing at the old air force base at Gimli, Manitoba.

Now, anyone who runs out of gas and sheepishly has to go looking for a gas station and a can of gas, is either a Gimli glider ot has pulled a Gimli glider." —Chris Thain, in *Cold as a Bay Street Banker's Heart: The Ultimate Prairie Phrase Book* Western Producer Prairie Books, Saskatoon, Sask., 1987.

give me a thousandth of an inch for play and a little drop of oil now and then and i will work 24 hours a day for you. I am machine. — *from a poem by T. S. Eliot or somebody* —graffiti on wall of sports car dealer shop (Whoever wrote this didn't have today's car in mind).

glass-packs — glass-packed mufflers, much in favor during the 1950s on cool cars, because they muffled engine noise to a smooth but noticeable harmonious sound, and when backed off, they allowed the backfire to sound through clearly. Also known as **hollywood mufflers, Smittys.**

GMC — officially General Motors Corporation, these letters mean "Garage Man's Companion" to some race car builders and fans because in the 1950s the GMC diesel trucks were the source of the first superchargers (**blowers**) easily available for transfer and adaptation to race car engines.

gnarly — "Valley girl"/ skateboarders California talk now applied to certain events during motorcycle racing. "It was, like, gnarly, man," the bleeding one was saying. "After I grabbed a handful of throttle, it spit me off the back, and I came down on all fours in these *rocks!*"" A situation where one may well suffer loss of skin or deformity (twisted limbs, etc.)

goat — the Pontiac GTO. Designer was John DeLorean, later famous for the now **orphan** DeLorean automobile and other old news.

gob of spit test — using materials near at hand, popular test for leaks at tire valve cores and air-conditioning valves. Spit makes a bubble if air is escaping. 100% reliable and accurate.

God's Bats — motorcycle gang in Austin TX in the 1950s-60s. See **Hell's Angels.**

you're **go for throttle up, Challenger** — since the NASA Challenger disaster, a customary way to say "go ahead and start it!"

go-go-mobile — tiny English car, like a refrigerator with windows and wheels. Makes ordinary humans inside look huge by comparison. An early, archetypal "go-go-mobile" was the Morris Mini, the first car in the world with rubber suspension. (Early entry by American car nut).
A British car fan who wishes to remain anonymous wrote after reading the above, "Gogomobil was German car produced by Hans Glas. 347 cc. engine (rear) under trunk. Squeeze 4. Roomy for 2. Went amazingly fast up Booley Bay Hill Climb in Jersey [Channel Islands] in top! -self at wheel. Have photo. Wish I had car. (And the **bubble** cars were smaller than the Gogo, which was smaller than a mini.)"

goil — gas and oil mix resulting from excessively flooded motor, fuel injection foul-up, etc. Does not lubricate nearly as well in yer crankcase as does oil. (Say you just had a fuel pump replaced.... and you check your oil....it smells of gasoline and is 1 & 1/2 quarts *over* the mark.....it's a safe bet that some gas has seeped past the fuel pump diaphragm into the crankcase.....(BMW Car Club Magazine *Roundel).*

"I filled it up" — she informs me, "and it only took 45 cents worth!" Jill was brand new to this VW. "Which place did you put it in?" I asked. "The back," she says, "I raised the hood and put it in where the little lid came off." To my horror, she takes me outside and points out the oil filler cap. I drain the oil/gas mixture, a black, thin, gaseous slime, add 30 weight oil, and it comes back to life.

"This car has never run better," Jill says, downshifting and pulling up the hill. "Do you think I should do that again sometime, to tune it up?" "Absolutely not," I reply. "Christ Shit Howdy, you nearly blew the engine, for sure. Believe me, don't do it again!"

goombah — GMBH, the Goombah Mercantile Company, American explanation of letters found on German products: actually "Gesellschaft Mit Beschrankter Haftung" — "Company with Limited Liability" or, "Inc."

go or blow — if "it's either go or blow," you've just rebuilt a motor and the time to start it up has come, or you are starting a racing car with a high-performance engine, or the warning light has come on and you need to get home. So you try it, and it'll either go or blow up.

gopher — or "gofer", lowest member on the team, the one who goes fer parts.

gorilla snot — gasket cement, such as Permatex #1 or #2, or maybe same thing as **elephant snot.** Also known as **lizard snot, leopard snot,** etc. "Yellow weatherstrip adhesive": —from Paul Burrill, Madison WI.

gorilla welds — a crude welding job, with too much slag.

go south on you — break down completely, suffer terminal engine failure. See also **eat its lunch.** In the Eastern Townships of Quebec, and in England, the term is **go west on you.**

grandma — low, low first gear on old American truck four-speeds, for moving off with a heavy load.

Grand Prix — movie, James Garner starring, good footage of actual road racing. First American racing film, maybe? (1959-60).

Grand Sport Corvette — built in 1960s to race against Carroll Shelby's Cobras. Lots of fun to watch (smoke boiling from rear tires, front end pulling wheelies upon acceleration, spin outs) but not terribly successful race car. Light, and godawful fast in a straight line, but un-aerodynamic and **tail happy** in corners.

gravel rash — skin condition caused by dropping your bike without wearing full leathers. See also **beef it.**

gravity starter — car that has to be pushed to start it.

gravy job — familiar task in car repair easily performed for a good fee. Exactly which repairs are "gravy jobs" is a trade secret of mechanics. "Polishing the valve covers" One mechanic we knew years ago once charged a gullible Jaguar owner $200 for this service, saying it would make the car faster.

grease — to slip the gears smoothly, as in "he greased it into second gear." Originally U. S. military, to run over and crush a small animal on the road ("I greased an armadillo last night").

how to **grease an MGB** — jack it up before you grease it. "It takes pressure off the kingpins, letting the grease go to the central wearing parts. It's the only way to do it."

grease — to run over and flatten out, as in "I greased an armadillo on the way home from the lake last night."

slicker than **greased owl shit** — a way to describe the surface on a motocross track or enduro trail when after one to two minutes of light rain, a clay surface turns slippery. May also be used to describe slipperiness of pavement after a light rain: oil residue, particularly in the part of the lane under exhaust pipes, makes the surface dangerous to motorcycles after a light rain. Wet leaves do it too.

grease monkey — an obsolete term for a mechanic. It is no longer in use, partly because recent cars do not have grease fittings. Modern mechanics like to be thought of as technicians, and they may be said to have earned the term, considering the complexity of the machinery they work on and the amounts of money involved. See also **parts changer.**
Grease monkey was a derogatory term, resented by mechanics. One story has it that a customer, recoiling from the grease-covered hands of his mechanic, said "You're dirty!" to which the mechanic replied, "Yes, but at 5:30 I'll be clean, and you'll still be ugly!" This story is a variation of a famous one told about Winston Churchill, who when someone said accusingly, "You're drunk!" he is said to have replied, "Yes ma'am, but in the morning I'll be sober and you'll still be ugly." ("Ugly" here may very well carry the sense more of "unmannerly, uncivilized" that it has in Nova Scotia, rather than "physically unattractive").

green — "non-polluting." "Rotary engines are 'dirty' burners of gasoline and very, very hard to make 'green.'" — *Bike* magazine, September 1990. A "green" engine is one precisely designed and engineered to perform with low emissions. Environmentally friendly.

"greenhouse" four-door hardtop — Chevrolet Belair, Impala, according to the Cool Car Club newsletter, Austin TX (Sept.-Oct. 1988). See also **"steamboat-bridge" rear windows, Vista, Holiday.**

green pea — new car salesman's term for an inexperienced buyer. "Everytime I see a customer, I see money." See also **New car salesman** and **upside down.**

gremlins — overheard from an ESPN sportscazster — "looks as if they haven't got all the gremlins out of Mario's car today, folks," as Mario's car mysteriously slows down on straightaway. A buzz word for "unspecified tuning problems." Definitely from Royal Air Force WWII.

grenading — yes, folks, it can happen, under the hood of your car. See **swallow a valve.**

greydog — as a verb, it means "to ship by Greyhound Bus express." "He said he would have them greydog the parts to his garage in the morning, and have me rolling by mid-afternoon." —from Jim Dodge, *Not Fade Away.*

greyhair — a senior bad driver, who makes unexpected and irrational stops, doesn't see what's coming, etc. Also **bluehair.**

gridlock — "We have gridlock," the helicopter reporter was saying. "All roads leading to and from the university area are jammed." Traditionally 8 am and 5 pm are times of gridlock (traffic jam).

ground effects — "In auto racing, the downward force created under the car. The underside of GTP cars is designed like a reverse airfoil and creates a powerful suction which holds the car on the road, a neat bit of engineering especially appreciated at speeds over 150 mph."

grunt-tight — tightening a bolt until it feels tight enough, rather than measuring the torque on it. Most mechanics over-tighten by about two percent. "Grunt-tight" is audible torque.

GTO — Gran Turismo Omologato (homologated, certified, regulated Gran Turismo). For different classes, x number of cars must be built for sale before they can compete.

GTP — Grand Touring Prototype. "'Touring' sounds quaint, if not ironic, but it comes from the early days of racing when touring cars were used." —from CHB. An anonymous British commentator: "not early, unless the 50s are early".

guibo — "drive doughnut", round rubber clyde....mounts/connects driveshaft to output flange of transmission in BMWs, Alfa Romeos, etc.

gull-wing doors — see **deLorean.** Or look at a Mercedes Benz SL 300!

gulp valve — see **pollution control devices.**

gumball machine — lights on top of a cop car. See also **cherry, firecracker.**

gumballs — "soft, compound racing tires, which don't last long but give lots of traction. Mostly used in qualifying."

gunk down — to hose down a greasy motor/ engine compartment with gunk, a degreasing agent, prior to high pressure wash. "Gunk it down and drive it to the car wash, buddy....."

gutless — having no power. Also, an Olds Cutlass in need of a tune-up.

H

hairpin — a sharp turn, i. e. near 180 degrees.

hairy — scary, dangerous, a close call. See **pucker factor.**

Hairy Davis — misspelling (no kidding) of Harley Davidson by an illiterate 19-year old inspector on an inspection sticker. When did apes first start riding motorcycles?

half a frontal lobe — "anybody with half a frontal lobe could figure this one out."

half moon — window rolled halfway down, see **full moon, pressed ham.**

halfshaft — British term for "each of the stub axles from differential to wheel."

half-ton honey — a girlfriend, not necessarily overweight, who **rides bitch** in your pickup. —from Saskatchewan.

Halon — a non-conductive powder which releases CO2 to extinguish all types of fires (A-B-C). Generally regarded as the best type of fire extinguisher material. Race tracks know about it.

Hammer — a fast, well-tuned Mercedes Benz 300 with a 5-6-litre engine, spoiler, and special suspension, named after a particular individual, Herr Hammer, who owns and runs a company which works on MBs to modify them for superior performance. The fastest production car made. Popular among West Texas ranchers, because they are capable of 180-190mph on the flat, straight roads in that part of the world.

put the **hammer down** — push the accelerator to the floor, downshift briefly if you have to, but in any case, open it **WFO!**

hand grenade — noun and verb. Certain air conditioning compressors self-destruct (heat, pressure, and lack of lubrication at start-up, all at the same time). "Handgrenade" describes what they are and what they do....fragments of metal sprayed in every direction....just be glad that they mount them under the hood and not between your legs.

hand on helmet start — one way to start a motorcycle race—with clutch out, engine running. See also **clutch start, Le Mans start, wave start.** —from Rod Root.

hang the ticket — to allow someone to charge car repairs, to do work on credit. "Sure, I'll hang the ticket, for two days only."

harder than assembling an old Chevy with metric tools — mechanics' metaphor of comparison.

hard luck class — motorcycle endurance racing trophy awarded to competitor who has had the worst luck that day (battered and bruised, ass in a sling). Has parallels in sailboat racing, etc....celebrating last place (usually an interesting picture (sight, story). See also **seat of pants class** (no instruments or computers).

hard parts — stuff not normally replaced due to wear. Fenders, bumpers, etc. Available only from dealership. See **soft parts.**

hardtail — the solid rear suspension, standard modification of a Harley to make it into a **chopper** along with long forks.

hardtop convertible — a car made to look like a convertible but with a fixed top. The key was the elimination of the side pillars between the front side and rear side windows. Not to be confused with convertibles with stiff, noncollapsible, removable tops, like the 1955-1957 Thunderbirds.

Harley tuning wrench — a hammer.

Harrison air — GM type air conditioners. Considered by most to be the best automobile airconditioning system (also installed as original equipment on Mercedes Benz, Rolls Royce, and others).

Hartge —foremost maker of performance equipment, e. g. four-valve per cylinder head with cam, carburetor or fuel injection setup for European cars. As in Hartge car, a German GTO.

haywire — obsolete? term for everything going out of control with a machine. See also **baling wire.**

headache bar — heavy metal grillwork in truck, designed to prevent load from shifting forward onto the cab and driver in case of a collision. From the *Dictionary of American Regional English,* citing Tak, *Truck Talk* (1981).

header — **custom** exhaust manifold.

head wedge — a mental block. "He's got his head wedged up his ass," said of a person who refuses to or seems incapable of understanding a fact about a car which has been repeatedly explained to him.

heat soak — technical term for buildup in temperature, to much higher than normal operating temperatures, due to sitting after running. Catalytic converters can run at 1750 degrees Fahrenheit, and other hot exhaust components, all of which are under car and hood, heat soak the rest of components of the motor compartment, thus raising their temperature beyond operating range, causing breakdown of solid state stuff, like General Motors electrical ignition module. —from the National Public Radio talk and car advice show "Car Talk."

heavium — fictional material of which exceptionally hard-to-lift items are made, like, e. g. the four-wheel-drive transmission. See **unobtainium, crudium.**

heavy Chevy — the Chevrolet with the big block, first the 396 in the Chevelle (1967), then the 427 cubic inch displacement motor introduced about 1969.

heel and toeing — in a car, blipping the throttle with the heel, **dab**bing the clutch, hitting the brake, at the same time, to downshift . —from D. H. According to Neil Hancock, SF author living in Austin TX, the term comes from the old MGs and Fiats and other sports cars with foot controls in close enough proximity to allow this adroit maneouvre with one foot.

Heinkel — Bubble car (see **gogomobile**), 1 front door, 3 wheels, 2-seat bench.

Helenomatic — a term coined by Bobby Richburg, Cedar Hill, Texas, in the 1950s, to describe his ease and comfortability in driving with his girlfriend (later his wife), who had learned to shift his gears (on a steering-wheel stick-shift car) while he was driving. Her name? what else but "Helen."!

Helldrivers — 1930s automotive stunt team on the carnival circuit, headed by **Chitwood and his brother.**

Hell's Angels — most famous and longest existing motorcycle gang in the world. Started among veterans in California after the

Second World War. Likely originally named after a squadron of Gen. Claire Chennault's Flying Tigers in Burma in the 1930s, who may in turn have been named for daredevil pilots in a movie made in that decade by Howard Hughes. Of course, the original Hell's Angel was Satan in John Milton's *Paradise Lost* (17th century England).

The names of motorcycle gangs tend to carry out this imagery: in Quebec, two of the biggest are the **Satan's Choice** and the **Devil's Disciples**. Our cartoonist Tony Bell was a member of a group called **God's Bats.** See also **one-percenter, two-percenter.**

hemi — original Chrysler Corporation design. Refers to the hemispherical combustion chamber shape.

herd it down the road — said of old cars driven by old folks, as you would a cow. Lots of play in steering wheel makes you correct constantly, thus the "herding motion."
Our anonymous British informant writes, "I've always called Morris Minor owners 'Leading Drivers' as they invariably led the (slow moving) column you were in. A pity, as it—the Minor—was a joy to throw round corners—a precursor of the Mini, which was even better."

hidden hinges — "Process of taking hinges that extend out of the side of the car and putting them on the inside so the hinge is hidden from view." —from Paul Burrill, Madison WI.

high beams — How will I get his attention? I'll forget to wear a bra...and show my high beams! —metaphor derived from car talk.

high-center — to run over an object in the road or path which sticks up enough to risk damage to bottom of car, oil pan, etc. "I had to be careful driving toward the river so I wouldn't high-center the car on a boulder and break the crankcase." —Norman Maclean, *A River Runs Through It and other Stories* (Chicago, 1976). Suggested by Eyvind Ronquist.

highly compacted spring — when you see this label on a mechanism, watch your face, do not drop. Learn how to recognize these components of struts, oil pumps, etc. Etched on a spring compressor at Poteet Motors.

high rise intake — air intake from up above, to drop fuel mixture into the engine with high velocity, for high performance. A **tunnel ram.**

high-sided, high-siding — if a motorcycle rider enters a corner at too great a speed, when the rear wheel loses traction and slides forward or even ahead of the front wheel, the rider may be "spat" off of the bike or "high-sided." The rear end steps out, slides, then gains traction and the bike spits the rider over the high side. Also, by analogy, **low side**, as in "to fall off the low side!" Front tire loses traction, bike falls over, rider falls on low side.

high tech — "a way of building a car with the latest and trick parts available. Often said to have had 'liquid money poured over it.'" —from Paul Burrill, Madison WI.

highway checkers — used to describe a situation in which one car switches lanes frequently on a two-lane superhighway, zig-zagging from lane to lane back and forth to pass slower-moving traffic. "He was playing highway checkers!"

high-winding — running the motor at very high **rpms**, really **revving** it, to get maximum speed.

hi mileage — phrase adapted from car talk to bar talk, to describe a hardened, bar-fly type of woman, an ex-prostitute, say: "she looks like she has hi mileage." "That one has some miles on her." "She has a facc like twenty miles of **bad road**".

hippie rig — like "jig-rig", a car dressed up with lots of toys, hanging decorations, etc. —from Terry Sayther of Phoenix Motor Works, Austin TX.

hog — a Cadillac (in black talk, as recorded and suggested to us by linguist William Labov). Also, and more commonly, a Harley motorcycle. "If it's got more than two cylinders it's Japanese!"

hog out — to crudely enlarge a hole. "Hog out that there hole, Bub..." Usually not with a drill, but rather a pry bar, jam bar, wedge, etc.

holed — this happens to pistons when mixture gets too lean....hot spot develops and 'fore you know it, burns a hole in top of piston crown, causing loss of compression, smoke, etc.

holeshot — the act of blasting off from starting line, at the drags, or of course, from the light. "You really got a good holeshot on him that time." The "hole" is an actual marked spot, with electronic sensors, within which cars have to wait for the signal.

Holiday — Oldsmobile **"greenhouse" four-door hardtop convertible** (1959-60). First of the Oldsmobile "Holiday 88s".

Holley carbs — original four-barrel carburetors for v-8 engines were made by Holley, one for each two cylinders. Think **gas-guzzler.**

Hollywood muffler — two Thrush mufflers spaced from the manifold at the proper distance so that the sound from each is perfectly in balance with the other. Also known as **glass-packs,** or at least they sounded mighty similar.

honking the horn — in Pakistan they honk at chuck-holes (pot-holes) in the road, i. e. at everything...... P. J. O'Rourke reports the same from Lebanon.

hood pounder — high pressure used car salesman (usually seen on TV, like the late Art Grindle of Dallas — see **out of sight guarantee**—who no doubt died of high blood pressure.)

the **hook** — the man who runs back the odometer, so you can sell the car and claim it hasn't been driven as far as it actually has, or so you can pay less at the car rental place when you bring it back.

on the **hook** — coming in on the tow-truck. Still called the "hook" even though modern tow trucks are equipped with the latest European "wheel lift" fork setup, which picks up delicate beasties by their wheels. "Captain Hook" is a widespread nickname for a towtruck driver who specializes in repossession or scrapping jobs: one of them in Montréal paints his truck black and displays the old skull and cross-bones pirate logo on the side.

Hooker headers — manifold made of tubular steel, not cast iron. Best, strongest, and could be tuned as to length and harmonic resonance, creating the music of the pipes. See "coming on the **pipes."**

hoopry/hooptie — "hoopry" is a slang term for "a car," in Calo/Cholo, or California Chicano English/Spanish dialect, according to Jennifer Waters in Jennifer Blowdryer, *Modern English: a Trendy Slang Dictionary* (Berkeley CA: Last Gasp, 1985), a dictionary of punk language. "Hooptie" is rap talk for "an old, broken-down wreck of a car that's just perfect for you and your crew." From Marvel's *Rap Dictionary*, 1991, as cited in "You got to be ampin'", Montréal Gazette, November 17, 1991.

uses for your **horn** — he had his hand on the horn button, ready. Driving slowly, he is watching a golfer nearby, looking, raising his golf club, and just as the golfer starts to swing, he leans on the car horn. The shot hooks badly, and there is suddenly a swish-swish-swish sound as the golf club comes boomeranging end over end in our direction. Just one in a series: Why should they play golf while we work?

horse hair — looks like horsehair, but the stuffing of auto seats which eventually shows up on the floorboard is made of glue and cellulose.

Horseshitsky Electronics — scrawled below "Hewlett-Packard" nameplate on piece of test equipment. Also inscribed:
"a) check power plug
b) **yell and hit it**"

hot goodie — flame from open exhaust or broken pipe. "The hot goodie melted the bottom of the passenger seat. I had to pull over and roll down the window and throw both dogs out and pour my beer on the burning carpet!"

a **hot New York second** — conventional way in Texas to say "an almost unmeasurable tiny fraction of time," defined in Ken Weaver's *Texas Crude* as "the amount of time it takes after the light turns green for a New York cabdriver to honk his horn at you."

hot rod — "An American-made passenger car which has been rebuilt or modified for higher performance and a distinctive, functional appearance....built primarily for straightaway speed or acceleration, such as lakes or drag competition, rather than for any form of road racing." —John Lawlor, *How to talk car* (Chicago: Topaz Felsen Books, 1965), *the* guide to hot-rod terms, with great old black and white photographs for illustration.

hotshoe — curved metal plate with metal toe, straps onto left boot in flat track racing (half mile) and short track (quarter mile) and the mile oval dirt track, to protect the foot while dragging it on the considerable length of curve. —from Rod ("Leadfoot," "Crash") Root, AMA Expert cardholder for motorcycle racing.

hot water 6 — the old Chevy 6 cylinder engine. Known to blow water hoses from time to time (going off like Old Faithful in the doing so). Also known as the **stove-bolt six.**

hot-wiring a car — to start a car, usually in order to steal it, without using the keys, by taking loose the wires to the ignition switch and connecting them directly. See also **Chapman lock**.

huarache — Mexican word for "rubber tire" and especially for "sandals made of cut-out strips of old worn-out car tire". Borrowed into English to say "all worn out, broken, used up" — "huarached out".

hunch back — hatchback.

hundred mile per hour decision — only you can make it, only you are in the driver's seat. Peter Keys, ace BMW mechanic and private test pilot, after working late, coming home at 3 am on freeway at 100plus mph, suddenly finds himself closing rapidly on unbelievably slow (55 mph) car in middle lane, his lane! Giving the turkey his bright lights (high beams) Peter curses, brakes hard, and watches turkey vacillate, waffle, feint going right, then go left, into the fast lane. It is too late. Peter has already swerved onto the far right lane and drifts past the 55 mpher sideways, all four tires crying.

I **hung it in his ass** — I sold him a car.

Hupmobile — 1930s car with an unusual "pre-selector transmission" which allowed driver to choose the next gear but automatically shifted it when the clutch was depressed. This feature was found on Daimlers and Lanchesters (even the pre-1910 L. had one).

hypo — high performance — "there's some hypo stuff in that tractor, Clem."

I

ice alert — device, original equipment on luxury European cars, which senses, through a bumper-mounted unit, temperatures below 30 degrees Fahrenheit, and flashes an amber warning light on the dash. BMW, among others, has in effect a built-in similar system in its onboard computer which, at the touch of a button, gives ambient air temperature, outside, and in event of freezing, blinks a little red light beside the temperature gauge, terrifying, in the process, new BMW owners. One of them called me after midnight to say, "There's a little red light blinking beside 'temp' on the onboard computer." "What does your engine temp gauge read?" I ask, yawning. "I don't know where it is," he replies. "Wait, I'll ask my girlfriend." He was gone for a minute, and upon returning, "She says it's in the middle." "Don't worry," I tell him, "drive home." The next day, we looked it up in his owner's manual, and there it was: "A red light blinking beside 'temp' indicates the possibility of freezing conditions on the road."

idiot light(s) — red/yellow lights that say things like CHECK ENGINE etc. —always too late to save it. Any light on the dash that replaces a gauge such as oil pressure gauge, water temperature gauge, or ammeter.

idiot-proofing — mechanics' term for a whole range of standard and optional devices and systems introduced into the modern automobile to try to keep people who don't know what they're doing from making disastrous mistakes, e. g. automatic transmissions. Another is the clutch-starter interlock, a switch installed on the Chevy Vega and others that doesn't allow you to start the engine unless the clutch is depressed. Buzzers tell you the key is still in the ignition, the seat belts aren't fastened, etc. In General Motors Firebirds, Camaros, etc., a new electro-mechanical device prevents your removing the key from the ignition until it is shifted into reverse gear. Thus the vehicle can't roll away when you leave the car.

A new device used fron 1988 is intended for **drunkproofing:** a bag the driver has to blow into and pass a breathalyzer test in order to get the ignition switch to work. **Childproofing** measures come under this heading, too: windows that don't roll all the way down, rear door locks controllable from the front seat, etc.

Nothing under the hood of a car is idiot-proof! For example, after touching or servicing an auto battery, wash hands to remove sulphuric acid residue before putting your fingers into your eye, etc. And you better believe it, buddy!

id. tx. — entry found scrawled amongst parts entries on big auto repair bill....when asked about it, he grinned ("it's an idiot tax.....this sonofabitch made me explain the dam job so many times...and bitched so hard about everything...I felt I had to compensate him for this abuse.") Another way to say the same thing: "Such ignorance should not go unrewarded!"

IFA — acronym on East German trucks in use in Nicaragua, which is locally explained as meaning "Imposible Frenar A tiempo" (impossible to stop on time)

illegitimi non carborundum — "the wrong part won't work"; also glossed as "don't let the bastards wear you down." The fact that this piece of bastard Latin is found scrawled on walls and in restrooms of shops and bars where mechanics hang out suggests both the level of education attained by some of them and the attitude of all toward precision in various fields of human endeavour. The Royal Air Force had it as "nihil illegitimum carborundum".

immaculate combustion — old energy transfer ignition. Where's the battery? It starts without one! An old Ducati 250 Scrambler was designed to both start and light up lighting with an energy-transfer ignition, which pulses an impulse to coil and points at just the right moment to make a spark. Thus the mystery—not a magneto, not battery operated, but energy-transfer ignition. Fitted also to old Triumph 500 twins.

impact detector — a sort of **deadman switch**, a mechanism which acts as cut-off switch in the event of a crash; actually a steel ball that rolls forward and upward slightly in a tube, and in event of severe impact, ball contacts two wires, thus energizing shutdown of fuel injection, minimizing danger of fire.

IMSA — The International Motorsports Association.

inbuilt jacking system — Old MGs had these. Simply put a brace in place opposite the side you want lifted, then engage the hydraulic pump, and it jacks up the wheel so the tire may be changed. Citroen still has such a system, using pneumatics (compressed air) instead of hydraulics (liquids). Daimlers and Lanchesters had it too, the "Jackall System".

Incision Motors — local name for Precision Motors (Dallas).

indicators — turn-signals (British car talk).

inertia wrench — a hammer. Also known as a **whop stick, Harley tuning wrench, fine tuner, Porsche hammer.**

inspection — check out carefully what you're ordering: "You can expect what you can inspect." —Lloyd Bentsen, October 5 1988, vice-presidential candidates' debate.

Instant Engine Overhaul — the can says....."Simply pour into crankcase & drive vehicle for 15 minutes.....Restores lost compression," the can goes on...."Stops smoking, seals rings, more power!" etc. (This can, now 15 years old, is presented annually, as an Xmas present, to one of our customers and employees who has the worst car (engine-wise) with smoking, worn rings, lost power—as a joke. No one has yet had the balls to pour it into a BMW! It has been refused/returned/thrown back 15 times.

intercooler — on turbocharged cars, "cools incoming air, making it denser and more effective. Racing turbos get plenty damn hot, almost red hot, so anything to cool the air down is welcome." See **vapor lock** remedy in South Austin.

Internal Hemorrhage — according to Bill Cosby, when the Kid is waiting at the lights with one foot on the brake and the other buried in the gas pedal, ready for the green, the automatic transmission is having an I.H.

invasion pliers — Large bolt cutters, available in various lengths. Invented for World War II, to cut thick wire easily and fast. With two-foot long handles and a pair of opposed cutting jaws, these babies will cut bolts in half up to about 1/2 inch in diameter.

Inventor of Night — see **Prince of Darkness.**

I-ROC — International Race of Champions, a competition organized for identical stock Camaros.

good old piece of **iron** — affectionate term for a solid, well-built American car, because of the extensive use of iron in them, before the days of aluminum and plastic. E. g. 1967 Chevy Impala. See also **modernized.**

iron horse — motorcycle. "Take the bull by the horns!"

iron butt — anyone who rides a motorcycle 100,000 miles. See *Iron Butt Association Newsletter,* ed. Michael Kneebone.

Isetta — made by BMW, tiny **bubble** car with one door opening to the front. Three wheels, sometimes 4—when a pair at back had a track of less than 12 inches. Neat little classic. Rich women fight over them at auctions. Extinct.

Isuzu parts — obtainable only through Buick dealers at considerable markup ($100 for a $25 brake rotor, etc.) Trade it in before it breaks.

Italian exhaust systems — (Ansa, Abarta, etc.) Have a distinctive sound. "Why does my BMW sound like a damn Fiat?" "It's that Italian muffler, sonny."

Italian tune-up — taking a machine out and driving it fast, really wringing it out, to burn out all the accumulated deposits in combustion chamber, etc. A necessary and accepted practice on Italian cars—Alfas, Ferrari, Fiat, etc.

itchy pussy — mechanics' jocular pronunciation of "Mitsubishi," as in the joke about the woman whose husband neglected her until she propositioned the grocery carry-out boy one day as they left the supermarket: "I have an itchy pussy!" "You'll have to point your car out to me, ma'am. All these Japanese cars look the same to me." —Jim Poteet and Greg Hirsch at Austin, Texas' International Car Parts.

Lest it be thought that all car jokes are about women, we must report that another nickname for the Mitsubishi is "Mr. Bitchy."

J

jacked up — main feature of a car with a lift kit suspension, to raise the rear end so that its powerful engine doesn't cause the rear to scrape on takeoff.

jackrabbit start — a quick getaway from the starting line in a race or from the green light in traffic.

Jane Dowling discount — performing a big job for absolutely free...or for dinner, simply because she (Jainey, twice) unbuttoned the top three buttons of her blouse...and leaned forward across the car and pointed out the problem with her Chevrolet. A classic instance of a mild use of the **couch and carry plan.**

jake-brake — an extra braking device on the tractor in some tractor-trailer rigs, which, using compression, restricts the flow of exhaust from the cylinders and increases the compression. The manufacturer is Jacob Mfrs.

jalopy — affectionate self-depreciating term for one's own old well-loved car.

Jap Jag — "Japanese Jaguar": a Datsun Z-series car. Also known as a **Z-car.**

Jap junk — term for any motorcycle not built by Harley Davidson, to the loyal.

Jap scrap — derogatory term for Japanese cars, which, like many such terms (**riceburners, fish-heads,** etc.), is no longer heard as their dependability is respected. Henry Ford is supposed to have said, "There'll never be a Jap engine in any car with my name on it," a vow that he kept but Ford Motor Company broke after his retirement. The change by which derogatory nicknames for Japanese cars disappeared no doubt produced many good stories, but one of our favorites is this one: as a response to the "invasion," the highly successful production and marketing of compact, efficient, low-gasoline consuming Japanese cars in North America, Pinto and Vega were introduced by Ford and GM respectively, with the hope that they would compete successfully with the Civics,

Datsuns, etc., not only Stateside but in the Land of the Rising Sun as well. Only somebody forgot to check the Japanese tax specifications, and the width of Pintos and Vegas put them in the top Japanese tax bracket, along with Jags and Rollses. Ooooops.

Jaws of Life — Rescue tool, hydraulically actuated spreading tool goes into metal to enlarge openings, open jammed car doors, so that trapped driver and passengers can get free of wreckage.

Jean-Pierre — see **Bombardier.**

Jeep — these little machines emerged during the late 1930s and came into their own during World War II. The name comes from the Army label, GP, for "general purpose".

Jersey barriers — in 1988 U. S. highway work, to keep all those long roads smooth and fast, the 8-foot long, 3-foot high concrete sections shaped to deflect cars with minimum damage, to separate traffic from work space. Concrete road dividers, they sometimes run for miles in northern Vermont. —Janet Green, Vermont Public Radio, October 4 1988.

Jesus pin — any small essential part which when dropped must be retrieved somehow. The mechanic says "O Jesus". Also known as the **O Jesus pin.**

jet off take — from Chuck Berry song "No Money Down." See **power brake.**

Jew canoe — Montreal talk for a Cadillac.

Jimmy — old nickname for GMC, cheapened by being made the model name of a 4 x 4. Also the name of the blower (supercharger) which came off GMC big diesels for use on early "slingshot" dragsters. See **GMC.**

jink — quick avoidance maneuver, usually to dodge small debris on road or track.

jitney — like **jalopy,** an affectionate, jocular term for a familiar old car. The term comes from "jit," probably from the French "jeter", "throw away", and was first applied to "cheap automobile buses" (according to H. L. Mencken's *The American Language*) which were presumably for hire for a nickel.

jobber — in other slangs, more generally known, the contractor who does specialized work, but in the world of car thief ring members, ...see **one day job.**

Joe Torque Wrench — the guy, one in every auto shop, who overtightens everything and consequently ruins lots of fittings, strips threads, breaks off bolts, etc.

John Law — a policeman. Also known as "the **man**", **Smokey.**

Johnson box — a solid-state device usually installed during federalization of imported cars (to make them comply with emission control standards). Wires are usually clipped or unplugged soon after installation, to restore European performance.

Johnson rod — phony part named to pad the bill for an unsuspecting and naive customer. Very, very expensive. See also **Johnson box.**

Jonah — a jinxed or unlucky car, a **lemon,** a car that brings only trouble in the form of repeated need for repair or lots of accidents. A Nova Scotia term, where it is pronounced "Joner."

joy ride — 1950s slang for "stealing a car." (You promised your girlfriend you would drive it back to the same neighbourhood....leaving it out of gas, of course.) Of course. See **test drive.**

the **Judge** — a Pontiac GTO with emission controls.

jugs — cylinders. "How many jugs does that one have?"

juice — usually "electrical current," but sometimes "gasoline." The active ingredient. (For a race car, the "active ingredient" is a good driver.

jump — to "jump-start" a car, to give the battery and electrical system a boost with booster cables from another vehicle.
— also, to start the car by pushing it and making the gears turn it over rather than the (inoperative) starter.

Junior Johnson — early famous stock car racer. Former Tennessee/North Carolina moonshine runner and good old boy who became one of America's fastest stock car racers. Junior Johnson's first super speedway win in 1953 in Darlington, SC came in a car that "was a liquor car a week prior to the race". —from *Car & Driver*, September 1992.

junk — even new cars bear this label. Low-bidder built, sub-designed, under-engineered machines. Let's name a few: Ford, GM, Chrysler, AMC.

K

Kahooten valve — like the **Johnson rod**, a mythical part which turns out to be very, very expensive to replace. "Well, you've lunched your Kahooten valve. We'll have to replace the engine."

Kangaroo Juice — Found in cars with touchy clutches, light gas pedals, and bad motor mounts—e. g. early thirties Austin 7s. Let clutch in too fast. Car leaps forward. Driver thrown back, lifts foot off gas. Car abruptly nosedives, so does driver, onto gas. Up nose, back driver, down nose—get the picture? Passage of car resembles passage of kangaroo or frog. (anon Brit.)

kidney buster — jocular term for a bus or truck with a particularly rough ride.

kill switch, kill button — see **master kill switch.**

kiss a fat man's ass — to eat it in a big way (have an accident).

kissed — jocular diminutive for "hit", collided with, though it usually means a minor bumping or **nerfing.** "Kissing the wall" in racing is "scraping the wall." —from CHB.

kit car — a reproduction, usually in fiberglass, of a classic, old, or fancy car. Also known as a **replicar. "Kit car"** is also used to refer to an auto "made by taking an existing model and adding a new body and a new interior," according to Francois Shalom, Montréal *Gazette* (January 15, 1990), such as the Spex, a souped-up version of the Honda Civic, and the Porsche Spexter, custom-designed by Paul Deutschman and Reeve Callaway (builder), the latter to replace 1990 Porsches whose design did not please customers (see **tree-frog**). The term was applied in a derogatory way to English Formula 1 cars by Ferrari because at one time they all used Cosworth engines in their own chassis and beat him!

kitty — Cadillac, also Jaguar.

kitty Cad — Cadillac coupe, in black talk.

kliks — usual spelling of **clicks (kilometers).**

kluged together — from a German word, slang verb for modern method of putting stuff together with clips (e. g. door panels, dashboards, trim, etc.) instead of with screws and bolts like God showed us how in the beginning. Drawbacks are that stuff breaks upon removal, or in attempts at removal, or springs apart by itself. In German, a 'klugler" is a wiseacre, an oversubtle reasoner, a sophist. What he produces is "klugelei"; both words represent ironic slants derived from "klug," clever.

knee-deep in rubber — has good tires. Used car term.

knee dragging — from motorcycle racing, teflon pads for the knee because under hard cornering, the racer hangs off the bike and sticks leg out, to shift the center of gravity. Aerodynamics, ballast, and feel are affected. You *feel* the lean angle. Practiced by **street squirrels** to show their machismo, though they are not cornering fast enough to need to **knee drag.**

knock — a disturbing engine noise, but it may not mean impending failure. Robert Appel, in *The Used Car Believer's Handbook,* defines it as "a sound like marbles dropping in a tin can" and says it is "what happens when the gas being used in your car has too low an 'octane' rating for the rated horsepower of your engine....Also known as 'pre-ignition,' it is not healthy for your car—the combustion chamber explosion occurs in the wrong part of the cylinder and the result is that tiny bits of the piston disintegrate each time the plug fires." British term is **pinking.**

knock it off the jack — mechanic's revenge on people who don't pay their mechanic bills. "If I ever see that car disabled by the side of the road, I'll knock it off the jack."

knock sensor — part of new generation electronic ignition systems. Little device senses "knock" or "ping" and electronically retards timing slightly, thus eliminating **knock** and possibly saving the motor.

knucklebuster — a nut that won't come loose for a long time, then, with extreme effort, it releases, drawing blood.

knuckle head — 1936-1947 Harleys, identified and named by the knuckle-shaped rocker boxes. See **flat head, shovel head, pan head, block head.**

Krautwagen, Krautmobile — any German car, long ago. Like **Jap scrap**, the performance and reliability of these cars drove out the derogatory slang.

kundenschmutz — German for "customer dirt." That's when the customer brings his car back, after you fixed something, and accuses you of screwing something else up, which you didn't do. Tricky situation (call your lawyer, tell them to go to your "special advisor"—Helen Waite.)

L

'labyrinth' seal — technically, oil or gas seal characterized by close fitting tolerances, a cut-thread spiral, drawing oil away from rather than toward the lip of the seal. Properly opposed piston compression rings form a labyrinth also, by forcing gases to go through a narrow ring gap and then around the piston and through yet another ring gap: a gas compression seal is formed.

Really, a "labyrinth" seal just fools the oil into running the other direction (overfill an MGA with motor oil by a quart or two and you will see that oil get smart).

Ladalac — heard on P. E. I., a grandiose name for a Lada that the owner is immensely proud of. Perhaps it should be spelled "Ladillac."

Lada trouble — what you get when you buy a Lada.

ladder bars — see **traction bars, wheel-hop.**

lake pipes — with dumps or cutouts controlled by cable from the driver's seat so these '60s era drag-street pipes' illegal noise could be turned on and off quickly if a cop was around. Very popular in their time.

lakesters — cars raced on Lake Bonneville, Utah, salt flats. As early as the 1950s, there were two-, three-, four-engine 300mph mothergrabbers doing this, driven by such as Colonel Goldie Gardiner, setting land speed records for cars with production engines, by using teardrop shaped bodies, bubble hoods for driver protection. A specially modified double overhead cam MG powered one early "lakester."

Lambo Rambo — the LM 002 four-wheel drive, 455 horsepower, $126,000 Lamborghini. Surely the fanciest of the sport-utility "off-road" vehicles available. 25 U. S. customers chose it in 1989. —*Wall Street Journal* (March 5, 1990).

Land Crusher — jocular name for the Toyota Land Cruiser. See also **Land Mark.**

Land Mark — jocular term for a Toyota Land Cruiser which has died and been left in a field.

land yacht — according to "Word Watch," by Anne H. Soukhanov in October 1989 *Atlantic*, "a large, elaborate automobile, typically one manufactured in the 1960s or 1970s." She also lists "greaser yacht" as an alternative form, and notes that mobile homes may be called "land yachts."

laughing gas — nitrous oxide, a fuel component used to boost power, sometimes known by its popular druggie name partly because it makes the driver and fans giggle at the stupendous power boost it produces. —from Erwin Schieder. See **nitrous rig.**

launch — to hit something low when you're going very fast, and you're ... launched...flying through the air, flipping, spinning, etc. —from *Road and Track*, Gran Prix racing and Dukes of Hazzard on TV).

Law of Untamed Consequences — a great unrecognized rule of modern technology. In the world of cars, one of its examples is that the elimination of lead from gasoline, to combat pollution, makes the engine not burn so hot; the hotter temperatures at which leaded fuel burned tended to combust away some oil deposits; thus the "cleaner" fuel is not always problem-free. Technology is full of examples of unintended side effects from "improvements," including the Dalkon shield and the Titanic, but many others came before them and no doubt others will follow. The classic moment of discovery of the Law of Untamed Consequences is contained in two lines of dialogue, unforgettable to anyone who heard them live: "You're *go* for throttle up, Challenger." "Uh-oh!"

Laws of Nature — more like the "fickle fingers of fate". Laws of nature dictate, among other things, that tires shall go flat when no compressed air is available, tornadoes will hit mobile home parks, brakes shall fail going down hill, etc. Shit happens. Very similar to Murphy's Law and other pessimistic universal visions/sets of rules. For the completely obverse view/ mindset, see **Don't worry/ be happy.**

laying rubber — gunning the motor, then letting out the clutch, making tires squeal and leaving a strip of rubber on the pavement. Also known as laying down **scratch** or laying down a **patch, peeling out, burning off.**

Lazy-Boy-Recliner — name applied to, aptly describing, the monster scooter Honda makes and calls the Helix—big, long-wheelbased scooter with laid back seating. Looks like a cross between a recliner and a U. F. O.

lazy J — rolling backwards and then **dumping the clutch**, causing the car to do a J-shaped **burnout,** leaving a J-shaped set of streaks on the pavement. See also **doughnut.**

lead foot — someone who habitually drives fast has a "lead foot," or **one foot in the carburetor.**

lead sled — heavy large American car before the days of aluminum and plastic—i. e. 1955 Buick Roadmaster or a '49 Merc. Often **chopped**. "A car customized, because the early customizers used lead, not body plastic, on the modifications." —from Paul Burrill, Madison WI.

lector scope — dashboard mounted, six or eight little neon bulbs, to monitor the spark plugs and tell you they were firing. Neat gimmick of the late '50s.

left-handed imbus wrench — we still haven't seen one yet. But it clearly states right here in the Hodaka workshop manual (factory manual) —"before splitting the cases, grip the clutch hub with the left-handed imbus wrench (to hold it still whilst unscrewing the hub nut)." We got it off anyway, holding or rather *rendering the hub motionless* by involving a shop rag in the gears. The "bus" part of the name of the wrench, which fits into a recessed groove in the center of a nut, stands for "Bauer und Schauerte", who were two German mechanic inventors.

Legalimit — "One of Rolls-Royce's few wholly unsuccessful ideas....a 1905 model with the stylish name of the Legalimit. Although it had a V8 3.5 litre engine, it was designed to be incapable of exceeding the legal speed limit of 20 mph. Only one was ever sold—to Sir Alfred Harmsworth, the press baron." —Fox and Smith, *Rolls-Royce: The Complete Works.*

Le Mans start — bikes on one side, racers on the other, and at signal, racers sprint to machines, and the start ensues. Named for the 24-hour auto race in France which uses this way of starting. See also **clutch start, hand on helmet start, wave start, dead start.** —from Rod Root.

lemon — a car that from the beginning has problems, because of faulty design or manufacturing. A car that became identified with this term, perhaps unfairly, was the Ford Edsel: its grille decoration had a shape in the middle that looked like a squeezed lemon. The French car Citroen bears a name unintentionally funny to North Americans: the word suggests "citron," "lemon." (This gloss of the name is denied by Gunther Full, a Michelin executive in Halifax, Nova Scotia).

Robert Appel, in *The Used Car Believer's Handbook* (Toronto: Dorset, 1979), defines a "lemon" as "a new car which doesn't work properly and which can't be fixed by any techniques known to modern science," and points out that "the manufacturers still like to deny the existence of" lemons!

letting the race come to you — "a strategy of driving a patient race and letting everyone else screw up." —from C. H. B. in the San Antonio *Current* the day before the San Antonio Gran Prix (1988).

lewitt — imaginary person or substance which aids the mechanic, in the jocular expression, "Nothing to it when you do it with Lewitt," accompanied by wiping hands off after completion of a tricky, hard-to-do task. See **tran-o-mite.**

lieutenant — see **weight watcher.**

lifetime warranty — ("for as long as you own the car") common nowadays on shock absorbers, brake pads, etc. Coldly calculated on statistics that indicate that modern men and women only hang onto car for three years. Warranties are nontransferable, mostly.

light up the tires — another term for **burning off**.

limousine liberal — someone who professes liberal principles but drives a big car. See **Cadillac commie**.

Linkum — no matter how much glitz they put into their advertising, big cars like the Lincoln Continental depreciate fast, and end up in front of old houses on the other side of the tracks. Hence the name change.....Linkum is a fully depreciated, or nearly so, Lincoln Continental—like over 50,000 miles, folks.

L L B — left lane bandit — a car which drives at or below the speed limit, hogging the left lane and preventing other drivers from passing it. —from Patrick Bedard, *Car and Driver*.

loaded — supplied with all possible optional equipment (e. g. air conditioning, tinted glass, AM-FM radio, etc.)

loaner — a car loaned to a customer by a body shop or garage during repairs, repainting, etc., on the customer's own car. A custom more widespread in car-blessed areas of the U. S., and in the good ole days, than it is elsewhere and now.

Locomobile — a quality family car, Buick class, of the 20s.

L. O. L. — little old lady. An expression of warning, that there is nearby an unpredictable slow driver: "Watch out, here comes a L. O. L!" First heard over the airwaves from traffic spotter in aircraft over San Francisco: "We have a L.O.L. blocking traffic on the Oakland bridge, folks."

loose — "when a driver turns the steering wheel and too much steering results, the car is said to be 'loose' or 'tail happy', also known as **oversteer.**"

loose nut behind the wheel — "We've located your problem, Mr. Wilson. It was a loose nut behind the wheel."
"That's why it wouldn't start?" he asks.
"It was outa gas," the mechanic says, grinning.....

lorry — British term for truck.

Lotus — currently little more than a label on the back of new Isuzus (Handling by Lotus). Lotus cars dominated Formula Junior racing in the 1960s and did pretty well in Formula 1, in the hands of Jimmy Clark, Mario Andretti, etc.

Lotus Super-Seven — true English sports car, light, low, and lean. 4-cylinders, 85hp, 700 lbs. "Perhaps the most like a sports car ever made"

lougan — racer who is not fast. "Beware of lougans off the line."

louvers — "a punched cut causing an area to be raised," for ventilation, as in hood. —from Paul Burrill, Madison WI.

low and slow — characteristic of the **low rider**: Jennifer Waters says that in one of these, "on a good cruise night, it could take up to 20 minutes to travel a block in the Mission District, from 23rd to 24th" in L. A.

low-balling — haggling with a car dealer for the lowest possible price.

low-end grunt — having lots of power at low rpms. Describes most American V8 engines. The opposite of **cammy, peaky, coming on the cam.**

lowering blocks — "blocks placed between spring and read differential causing the car to sit lower." —from Paul Burrill, Madison WI.

low rider — a chopped and channeled car which has an electrically operated hydraulic pump suspension system instead of shock absorbers, so that at stop lights, the whole car may be raised and lowered dramatically for effect, making it appear to hop. In the Calo/Cholo (California Chicano slang) section of her punk dictionary, Jennifer Waters defines it as "a car rigged up to lean to the front or rear end to an extreme degree. If this vehicle is not already slow enough, it can then be made to bounce up and down or come to a dead halt if the driver spots a passing acquaintance on the sidewalk." —*Modern English: a Trendy Slang Dictionary* (Berkeley CA: Last Gasp, 1985).

low-sided — if a motorcycle rider enters a corner at too great a speed, and loses traction on the front wheel, the bike usually just falls over and the rider is "low-sided." See **high-sided, high-siding.**

L-plates — Known as "destination plates," red "L" on white background. Legally required in the U. K. on all vehicles, front and rear, when driver has a "provisional licence" ("Learner's Permit" to you, yankee). (Anon. Brit.)

lugging — trying to accelerate while in too high a gear to have any power, straining the motor and gearbox.

lunching — causing another part to disintegrate totally. See **eat its lunch. Unglued, fiended, cooked.**

lying in the weeds — said of a motorcycle cop waiting to catch speeders by hiding behind a billboard (on the old 50s four-lane freeways), or of a high-performance car which is not visibly a **bad boy car** so that it outraces unsuspecting fellow drivers by driving **WFO** unexpectedly.

M

macadam — a word for a form of pavement, originally a cyclist's word, as it was a cyclist, a Mr. MacAdam, who first invented pavement.

machine — car such as a Porsche 957, a Lamborghini Countach, capable of 320 kilometres per hour, without rolldown windows, etc., designed to go fast without creature comforts.

Mack — Mack Truck. One with little chromed bulldog on hood. Tonnage. Yield to tonnage.

maggot wagon — workers' term for the lunch or break-time portable canteen truck which pulls up to construction sites and mechanic shops and sounds its horn. See also **roach coach.**

mag wheels — first developed for racing cars by Tulio Campagnolo, of racing bicycle fame, as a streamlining feature.

make and break engine — early marine inboard motor, magneto ignition, massive, heavy, big flywheel. The name comes from the ignition which has, in effect, the contact points for ignition inside the combustion chamber, combining the functions of the spark plug and the ignition points.

Legend in Nova Scotia and Maine has it that fishermen would use them for anchors, then, when required, haul them up, run some oil through them, start them and use them to drive the boat!

Farley Mowat offers a classic description and an alternative opinion: "She was a seven-horsepower, single-cylinder, make-and-break, gasoline-fuelled monster, built in the 1920's from an original design conceived somewhere near the end of the last century. She was massive beyond belief, and intractable beyond bearing. In order to start her it was first necessary to open a priming cock on the cylinder head and introduce half a cup of raw gasoline. Then you had to spin her flywheel which was as big as the wheel of a freight car and weighed about the same.

"There was no clutch and no gear box. When, and if, the engine started, the boat immediately began to move. She did not necessarily move forward. It is an idiosyncrasy of the make-and-breaks that when they start they may choose to turn over either to left or right (which is to say either forward or astern), and there is no way known to man of predicting which direction it is going to be.

"Once started, the direction can be reversed only by snatching off the spark-wire and letting the engine almost die. On its next-to-final kick it will usually backfire and in the process reverse itself, at which instant one must push the spark-wire back in place and hope that the beast will continue turning over. It seldom does...

"According to mythology the virtue of these engines lies in the fact that they are simple and reliable. Although this myth is widely believed I am able to report that it is completely untrue. These engines are, in fact, vindictive, debased, black-minded ladies of no virtue and any non-Newfoundlander who goes shipmates with one is either a fool or a masochist, and is likely both." *The Boat Who Wouldn't Float* (McClelland and Stewart, 1969, chapter 7).

For a description of another make-and-break engine, see **flutter valve.**

I didn't **make it and I didn't dream it** — retort given to whining, sniveling car owners by mechanics and parts men after the delivery of bad news. Also, sign on wall of auto repair shop: "**No Sniveling, No Whining**."

the **man** — a policeman. See also **Smokey, John Law.**

man's best friend — the original vise-grips, made by Petersen Mfg.

marbles — from flat track racing, "he's in the marbles" refers to the higher, wider part of the curve, as opposed to the **groove** — "marbles" refers both to the small bits of stuff thrown to the outside and to its relative lack of traction.

Martian piss — bright green hydraulic fluid they use in the suspension systems of Citroens.

Masers, Maserati — some idea of the pace and atmosphere of the road in Italy may be derived from a story about a celebrated murder trial in that country. A Fiat passed a Maserati, they say, and the driver of the Maserati was so annoyed he speeded up, drew abreast of the Fiat, and blew away the driver with his gun. When he was brought to trial, the judge threw out the case, saying, "Everyone knows a Fiat cannot overtake a Maserati!"

master kill switch — required on all race cars and bikes, as well as a big decal identifying it, so engine and all electrics can easily be shut off in event of a crash, by either driver or rescue personnel.

maypops — used car term for unguaranteed tires. "She has a good motor....and maypops for tires." Since used cars sit around and rubber gets fatigue from the sun and rain, and just sitting in one spot (flat-spotting), even good looking, deep treaded tires can be of the "maypop" variety.

coming on the **mega** — a British way of saying "coming on the **pipe**" when megaphone pipes were all the rage on hot bikes. "Like a kick in the pants."

megaphones — cone shaped exhaust tips.

melt down — a massive short in a car's wiring, usually accompanied by lots of smoke, crackling noises, melted wires and plastic, etc. Run, don't walk away from stuff like this. Call the fire department.

Mercedes star — hood ornament. These chrome goodies, sticking up from each Benz, make great roach clip handles....like watermelons and kisses, most cherished when they're stolen.
Mercedes was named for Otto Benz' daughter. He invented the four-stroke engine, and built maybe the first functional automobile, in 1876-8? - called the Otto Cycle.

Meskin resort feeling — to have the benefit of hearing jungle construction equipment roaring, pounding, and scraping while you eat breakfast. See also **big city feeling.**

Meskin tape — by a slight deliberate mispronunciation, "masking tape" becomes "meskin tape," especially in South Texas, where Mexican workers do most or all of the tedious, painstaking body work, starting with applying masking tape to surfaces that must be kept clean when the car is spray-painted, like windows, molding, trim, etc.

Messerschmidt — **bubble** car, tandem seats (2), 3 or 4 wheels.

methedrine-hamster engine — mythical comic motor powered by a rotary hamster cage treadmill with the hamster fed a steady supply by eye-dropper of methedrine ("speed").

metric — "Speed Limits Are In Metric" -you will see this unusual sign entering Canada. Farther down the road, there will be one that reads Speed Limit 100. You will see neither of these signs in the U. S., yet.

Mexican overdrive — putting the car in neutral while coasting down hills, presumably to save gas. Akin to "Mexican breakfast" ("a piss and a cigarette")

Mexican speed wrench — a channel-lock pliers. In Ohio, it is known as a **West Virginia speed wrench.**

Mexican traffic light — a speed bump. Also known as an **axle destroyer, bumper remover**

Mfrs. — abbreviation for "Manufacturers." Sometimes read off packages as "motherfuckers."

MG — Morris Garages, maker of the car. The first MG was a modified Bull-nosed Morris. "Mr. Morris didn't talk to Mr. Nuffield back then." Later powered by Austin engines. See **MOWOG.** Eventually a part of British Motors Corporation, with Jag, Morris, Austin, British Leyland.

I see that you dropped a **Michelin detector** — he said, leaning over to pick up the large screw.

Michigan markers — the lights on the corners of the box of large freight trucks. No doubt from the large number of highway trucks that were licensed out of Michigan.

Michigan stop — a rolling stop. See also **New York stop, American stop, Hudson stop.**

Mickey Thompson — famous drag racer, Indianapolis 500 racer. Also known for Mickey Thompson mag wheels.

middle finger salute — insulting gesture which attempts to revenge one's being nosed out in a right of way dispute, etc. Leads to violence occasionally, especially when it is offered by the winner in addition to the victory.

Mille Miglia — Italian for "thousand miles," a famous/infamous road race in Italy, cancelled forever due to great number of deaths incurred when cars crashed into crowds, cows wandered onto road, etc. Nevermore.

Milwaukee vibrator — a Harley-Davidson motorcycle (made in Milwaukee).

mini — the Austin "Mini," a tiny British car sold for a time in America, but which failed, some say, because it was too low — "bumpers ran over it." For a British opinion, see **herd it down the road.**

minoune — a Quebec French term for a big, unwieldy car, a **pig, boat, land yacht, yank tank,** or **snowbanker. "Minou"** is the Quebecois term for "cat." A "minoune" is a fat female cat. See also **chaloupe.**

mint — like new, **cherry, virgin.**

missing — not firing on all cylinders, because of valve or ignition problems. Pre-ignition can be caused by bad gas, improper timing, etc. Also known as **skipping.**

Model A heater — hand-made sign on a car cushion in the back seat of Everett Arey's 1930 Model A Roadster, Upper Port Latour, Nova Scotia, 1988.

modernized — now made of plastic. **Ultra-modernized** means "now made totally out of plastic."

module — in car talk, a solid state device (which may fail after every three years in yer Datsun truck, costing you $300), and which if you bash one open, it looks like it has a little town inside it, without people.....little houses, watertowers, condos, cops, streets, bridges, etc. You don't fix modules; you buy a new one.

monkey motion — "imprecise or excessive motion in any mechanical device, ...e.g. a carburetor linkage or gear shift lever." —from John Lawlor's *How to talk car*. Technology has left this term behind, so that it is somewhat obsolete, except for people who continue to work on, race, drive old cars.

monkey suit — work uniform (or business suit). Conformity breeds contempt. Mechanics in Texas especially loathe these. Usually made of polyester, which doesn't breathe like cotton, uniforms are hot and hated.

throw a **monkey wrench in the gears** — figurative expression for sabotage or self-destruction of "best laid plans" etc. See **Murphy's Law.**

monocoque — unibody construction, i. e. frame consisting of reinforced and welded-up sections of stressed metal skin. From aircraft. When you can poke a Bic pen through the unibody frame section, the car is a **salad bar.**

moon — a verb meaning to show one's naked ass to a car that one is passing. See also **pressed ham, full moon, half moon.**

moons — little shiny round hubcaps (Nova Scotia). Actually, a Dean Moon was the designer of the first "moon" hubcaps, which were aerodynamically streamlined for airplanes, then used on **lakesters.** They were made of spun aluminum, which was stronger than other metals of the time, and were slightly dished.

moon discs — shiny, bullet-like hubcaps for 1950s-1960s cars. See also **disc wheels, moons.**

mopar — "motor parts," Chrysler Corporation's own parts company.

mosey — old expression from horseback days that describes slow but purposeful movement. Those old duffers still drive their Buicks and Chevs that way. "Let's mosey on into town, Mom." "Let's mosey on down the road a piece."

motate — a very common word, "to roll on down the road." "How's yer car?" "Oh, it's motating along all right." Possibly a "stunt word," formed from "motor" and "rotate"?

yer **mother's car** — "Hell, you could drive yer mother's car down that road," said of University of Texas caver (cave-explorer) about Mexican road into the mountains. Your mother's car, by inference, is a low, wide Buick or big Chev, etc.

Moto-Guzzi — famous for making the most dramatic of the **screamer** racing machines, a V-2 850cc, 150 horsepower motorcycle.

motorbike with doors — early insulting phrase to describe compact Japanese cars, some of them built by makers of motorcycles, like Honda.

motor crap — slang term for "Motorcraft", subsidiary of Ford, maker of spark plugs, etc. for Ford Motor products.

Motronic — Bosch (electronic parts co.) trade name. Late 80s BMWs are Motronic in this sense: idiot-proof almost. You can't reset the timing or a lot of other stuff because it's totally contained by computer (sensors emerge from computer, go to various places on the engine....no adjustment is provided). Eliminates the possibility that the kid down at the gas station could run the timing ahead, etc.

mouse — a small-block Chevrolet, as contrasted with a **rat.** — from Erwin Schieder.

mouse trap — (a) early Harley clutch throwover linkage-box thing. (b) old Ford starter design, of doubtful value. Remote starter solenoid activated mouse-trap apparatus which engaged bendix with flywheel....or didn't....or made funny "ching" sound, depending on the weather or other acts of God.

mouse soup — STP engine oil additive which thickens it. According to Robert Appel, "several years back Consumer Reports did a feature [which claimed that] STP was simply an overpriced viscosity modifier and might provoke the manufacturer to void a new car warranty. The day the article appeared, the price of STP stock plummeted. However, the public has a short memory and the stock and product are both doing nicely now, thank you very much." —*The Used Car Believer's Handbook.*

moving chicane — "a bad, reckless, or dangerous driver." See **chicane.**

mowing the lawn — see **picking daisies.**

MOWOG — mysterious inscription cast into metal on almost all parts of the engine of the MGB, engine block, exhaust manifold, transmission case, etc. Howard Scoggins, veteran foreign parts man in Texas, says it stands for the five towns or villages where the castings are done: Morris, Oxford, Wolseley, etc. The less well-informed mechanics' folklore explanation is that Mowog was the nickname of a hard luck mechanic who worked on nothing but MGBs, bought lots and lots of parts for his race MGB, and never finished a race, always breaking down...... In fact, it stands for MOrris WOlseley Garage.

muddin — going out driving in a muddy field and thus trashing the appearance of your four-wheel drive, doing **donuts** in slippery mud. Guess what this does to the field!

muffler bearing — phony part named to pad the bill for an unsuspecting and naive customer.

muffler damage — "I loosened the muffler going over a bump," she says, handing me the keys. "Would you fix it? I don't think it's very bad."

"I'll take a look," I say.

Her boyfriend called a few minutes later, with the story. "There were four or five of us in the car," he said, "all drunk. And she couldn't see the road divider, and we climbed it at 50 mph and rode it for about 100 feet...down the middle of the road. Sparks were flying out the back, the bottom of the car must be ground off at least an inch. Check it out."

The bottom of the car looked like a giant belt sander had been applied to it. The muffler was dangling, in terminal shape. I called her back at the office.

"Did you see someone driving down the median on Anderson last night?" I asked. "It was spectacular...sparks flying...everything....just like the fourth of July."

Silence on her end.

"Kevin called you," she said quietly. "I'll get even with him for this."

Muntz Jet — made in California in the 1950s, powered by a supercharged Cadillac engine, this production car was made in limited quantities, would reach 0-50 mph in 6 seconds, still fast. Named for inventor Mad Man Muntz, who had helped Kaiser built Liberty ships during the second world war.

Murphy's herpes — the rust on a car that is so bad in every way that "anything you did to it created another problem. From "Murphys Law."

muscle car — fashionably large, heavy, powerful, low car during the 1970s and 80s, e. g. a Ford Mustang. A car designed for driver and passenger comfort modified by the addition of a powerful engine (though the way they're driven tends to sling passengers around if they don't buckle up and hang onto the hand-holds). See also **test drive, Studelack.**

Doug Petcau of Montréal says they're making a comeback, in the form of the ZR1, a new $50,000 Corvette, here in the early 1990s.

mush-matic shocks — old and worn out.

MV — the legendary, now classic MV Augusta motorcycle (Italian), reknowned for the beautiful, almost musical-instrument shape of its exhaust pipes, two on each side. One of the first racing 4-cylinder motorcycles, but did not antedate the AJS V-4 watercooled supercharged 500cc bike that first lapped the Isle of Man at over 100 mph in 1939.

N

nail it — accelerate. Also known as **floor it, floorboard it, hotfoot it, stand on it, launch time, peel rubber.**

how to **name a car** — "How is your car?" I ask, inquiring about her inheritance from an aunt, a classic light blue and white two-tone Olds 88. "Oh," she answers, "you mean my 'Olga' — my uncle named her." The rule of thumb is "the first letter of the name must be the same as the first letter of the brand name of the car." "He had a 1948 Dodge named Dorothy." "Ford Francis", etc.

National racing colors — developed for Formula I racing, they are light blue for France, green for Britain ("**British racing green**" is a name for a color widely known), red for Italy, silver for Germany, and white with two blue stripes for the United States.

The distinctive tone of British Racing Green comes from the time when a team of factory Napiers (?) went to race in Ireland, early in the century. In honor of the country, they were painted green. But green is unlucky, so it was nearly black to fool the fates. It caught on and was known evermore as B. R. G.

nerf — to nudge someone from behind while speeding down the highway.

nerf bar — one of two solid pipe bumpers, set vertically rather than horizontally, for "nerfing."

stuck in **neutral** — this problem is older than cars: "unable to get an erection."

a gearbox full of **neutrals** — said by James Hunt, commenting on a Formula I race in which Petrazzi had just blown a transmission: "He's found a gearbox full of neutrals!"

New Brunswick credit card — a length of rubber hose, for siphoning out gasoline from someone else's filler pipe. See also **Oklahoma credit card.**

new car salesman — at the local Austin TX Mercedes dealership didn't recognize Willie Nelson at all. Clad in jogging clothes and his famous headband, he had strolled into the showroom, looked around, and was sitting behind the wheel of a blue full-size Mercedes sedan.

"Hey, hippy," this salesman, Louie, I think his name was, said, "What're you doin' in that car."

Not taking any offense, Willie gave the salesman a beatific smile of the sort that only mega-rich rock and roll stars have. "I was thinking about buying it," Willie replied.

"And how would you be paying for it," the salesman asked sarcastically. Unflappable, Willie wiggles the steering wheel, pretending to drive it. "I guess," he replied, "I'd just call my friend David down at the Austin National Bank, and have him transfer you the funds. Can you have it ready by 4:30?"

Something snapped inside the salesman's brain. "Let me," he replied, suddenly a lot more courteous, "get my sales book."

His co-salesman, back in his office, sniggered at Louie, who was frantically assembling his pens and forms. "Don't you know who that hippy is?" he whispers. "That's Willie-fucking-Nelson, and he isn't even asking you to come down any on the sticker price."

"Oh, Jesus," Louie gasps, "that's $2000 for me....Oh Jesus."

It totally bent the guy, selling Willie that Benz, Greg reported. For a month and a half he would see someone in t-shirt and gym shorts coming across the parking lot, and...."here comes another one," he would exclaim, leaping up from his desk. He would intercept the guy. "Hi," he would say, "would you like to test drive the new 450 SL...it's very fast...comfortable too...."

"No, thanks," the guy would inevitably reply, "I just need a fan belt for my old '66 190 diesel."

The specialized vocabulary—the lexicon—of the world of new car salesmen is explored in an essay by Greg Goldin published in *Doctor's Review* (August 1989), which explains that "the box" is the showroom foyer where with the help of the "foursquare" (the worksheet) and their wits and words, a clever sales team can sell a car to almost anyone, sometimes managing to "pack the payment" ("leave little breathing room between what you've said you'll spend and what in fact you owe"). Goldin's definition of the six-fold classification of potential buyers is masterful:

Grinder — one who tries to wear down the salesman on price. A good salesman will have this person outflanked six ways to Sunday.

Jackoff or **Stroke** — one who is shopping, not buying. Regarded with all the respect implied by the nomenclature.

Laydown — a patsy. A lamb to the slaughter. One who will buy no matter what the cost. An obvious favourite with salesmen.

Mooch — one who won't settle for less than a good deal. Universally hated. "This prick is trying to steal from us," observes the sales manager.

Payment buyer — one concerned primarily with monthly payments. Salesmen pray for (and prey on) this type; they make up 70 per cent of new car purchasers. A payment buyer is a laydown on the installment plan.

Roach — A bad credit risk (not necessarily a bad person to sell to).

Goldin quotes the new car salesman's oral rule number one, which says more than it seems: ***buyers are liars.***

See also **upside down, green pea, note lot**, and **outrun the note.**

Newfie Toronado — a 55 Chevy with snow tires on the front wheels.

New York stop — see **rolling stop.**

NG, NDG, NFG — various levels of broken, as in No Good (slightly broken), No Damn Good, and No Fucking Good (really broken). Also known as **knackered** (from the term used for the person who bought old horses and turned them into dog food, in the old days), **effed, buggered.**

nibbler — a jocular diminutive term for an unusual tool which is handy in solving some unusual mechanic's problems: a pneumatic metal scissors with which the man can eat his way through to a problem area, chewing through all kinds of metal obstacles.

nine — A Buick Electra 225, in Black talk (add up the numbers and you get 9). —Leonard Zwilling, staff member, *Dictionary of American Regional English.* See also **deuce and a quarter.**

nitro — nitromethane, a dragster, especially **fuel dragster**, fuel. To be distinguished from **nitrous**, or "nitrous oxide," **laughing gas**, which also is a fuel component used to boost power, but in less dramatic fashion and in a wider range of vehicles.

nitrous rig — a car with nitrous oxide injection, against the rules in racing and dangerous in any car, because once it is turned on, it cannot be turned off or throttled down until the nitrous oxide is all consumed. See the movie Road Warrior for a demonstration on straight roads.

no ferro dulce — Spanish for "no sweet iron", part of an observation by a Mexican mechanic on looking at a ruined bearing race (the part the balls roll in)....

Nomex suit — flameproof protective suit worn by race car drivers.

non-demountable rims — a feature of the 1914 Ford Touring car. Wheels could not be removed. Norman Baylis, of Montreal, says he had to pry the tire off the wheel, remove and repair the inner tube, and pry the tire back on! To fix a flat!

normally aspirated — a racing term for an engine which is not turbocharged. Aspirate — breathe.

Northern speed wrench — a pair of torches (two gas nozzles, for mixing oxygen and acetylene, for cutting and welding).

nosed — modified at the front of the hood. —from Paul Burrill, Madison WI.

nosey — said of long-nosed cars such as Datsun Z cars, E-type Jags. May also refer to their nose-heaviness and thus tendency to **understeer.**

No Sniveling, No Whining — sign on wall of auto repair shop. See "I didn't **make it and I didn't dream it.**"

notchback — indented trunk.

note lot — slang for a sleazy car lot that finances its own cars. "We Tote the Note." "Don't walk See Hawk".

nothing comes from nothing — an old Latin (Roman) saying, this phrase comes to mind when listening to two young motorcycle racers discussing the piston damage to an RZ 350 which had run low on oil in the fuel-oil mix: "I wondered where that aluminum came from!" — upon discovering a glitch in the piston.

Nova — this Chevrolet compact car was the butt of an enormous unintentional miscalculation: those responsible for naming it didn't notice that marketing it in Latin America would result in much merriment, because No Va means "won't go" in Spanish. According to Robert Appel, the Cadillac Seville has been called a "$14,000 Nova." —*The Used Car Believer's Handbook.* For a similar story, see the story of the name of the Silver Mist under **Rolls.**

to go **Nova** — to burn as a result of leaving the choke on too long on a car equipped with a catalytic converter. These systems run at

1250 degrees Fahrenheit; when the choke is left on too long, lots of raw gasoline is dumped into a unit directly under the floorboard designed to burn only leftover gases, and the undercoating and floorboard catch fire.

Nurnburgring — famous German auto racing track, now disused as "too dangerous".

nut cutting — changing performance equipment for stock o. e. m. (original equipment manufacturer) same as your car came new with.

nylon thump — see **flat-spotting.**

O

obgefucked — fucked up. Germ-Inglish word (ist nicht Deutsch, und ist auch nicht Englisch—would be "ab-gefuckt" if were even close). See also **dis machinen ist nich fur der gefingerpoken etc.**

oceanliner body job — a very bad repair job on the car body, unintentionally not smooth or straight. "I don't want a wave machine!"

octane booster — Mothballs in the gas tank break down and provide a nitro-like increase in octane. This phrase is also a term derived from car talk used to say "cocaine", along with "rocket fuel." There was in early days an additive for low-octane gas which would inhibit the reaction of gasoline to air, delaying combustion to higher temperatures, to prevent pre-ignition, **knocking.**

off-road fire prevention pipe — a special Y-shaped exhaust pipe with a cutout valve, bypassing the catalytic converter, on **bad boy cars.** See also **butane rig.**

oil-burner — a car which is still barely running despite worn piston rings and cylinder walls. The wear allows oil to mix with the fuel mixture and burn, producing clouds of dark smoke from the exhaust. Also a term for a diesel-powered vehicle, because they naturally release smoke from oil combustion. See also **roadfogger.**

oil company tool box — nothing but wrenches three feet long, none of the gauges read below 2000 psi.

oil leaker — Porsche. See also **overturned soup spoon, first at the site of the accident,** etc.

Oklahoma credit card — a length of rubber hose, for siphoning out gasoline from someone else's filler pipe. See also **New Brunswick credit card.** One might think, from the occurrence of these similar phrases in very different regions (Texas, for the "OKlahoma c. c." and Nova Scotia, for the N. B. c. c.), that it is a nearly universally known phrase. Our research does not support that idea. And the two regions in which we have found it are similar, we find, in that the people who live there are by and large not only less well off in money than their scoffing neighbors, but ridden also by a certain lack of pride, by comparison with the neighbouring province or state. Texans are known for their bragging; Nova Scotian pride has a certain fierceness. Oklahomans and New Brunswickers have to survive somehow.

old pilots — from aviation, "there are old pilots, and there are bold pilots, but there are no old, bold pilots." Applies to automobile and motorcycle drivers, too.

Olds — "Ask the man who owns one" was an early and longtime advertising slogan.

o-matic — Ford-o-matic, Turbo Hydra-matic, Cruise-o-matic, Select-o-matic, Powerglide, Torqueflight, are all trade names for automatic transmissions. Some names, like Cruise-o-matic, were green lit in plastic in the middle of the dash, announcing, no doubt, once again this year, an improvement on the wonderful automatic transmission. See also **Vacuumatic, Suck-u-matic, flush-o-matic.**

omigod — nickname of the Plymouth Omega, only one in a series of god-awful domestic-built cars that seemed to gush oil from various sources.

Omnirizon — the Omni/Horizon family of Chrysler products. See **badge engineering.**

On Any Sunday — I and II. Bruce Brown's famous documentary films of motorcycle racing, with Steve McQueen and others.

one day job — also known as a **jobber**, this term is applied by car thief rings to cars that can be cut up, distributed, and sold in one day. See **chop shop.**

one foot in the carburetor — someone who drives fast has "one foot in the carburetor."

one for the road — traditional justification for a beer or a toke, this practice is ill-advised in the current state of law enforcement. It does suggest that America's love affair with the road is sometimes bumpy or boring, just like other long-term human relationships.

that car needs **one of everything** — expression applied to a worn out car.

"It just needs a battery and tires, Dad."

"It needs one of everything!"

one-percenters — macho variation, used by Hell's Angels, on the **two-percenter** self-applied label adopted by many bikers after the head of the American Motorcycle Association declared in the early 70s that "98% of all motorcyclists in America are decent, hardworking, lawabiding citizens."

one wheel in the sand — a term used for someone who is acting as if he is mentally deficient or disabled. See also "not hitting on all **eight.**"

on the cam — "the range at which the engine is at its best performance." —from C. H. B. in the San Antonio *Current* the day before the San Antonio Gran Prix (1988).

open it up — two meanings: 1) to accelerate to top speed, or 2) to wound oneself during work on a car.

Opel — built in Bochem, Germany, near the Krupp factory, an area bombed flat by the Allies in WWII. Opel parts only obtainable through General Motors at considerable markup, effectively rendered the little cars to **orphan** status. Wrecking yards don't retain Opels very long before compacting them into little square steel bales, for meltdown.

opie switch — parts man's term for "oil pressure switch," because the box is marked "O/P switch."

orange peel paint job — a very bad paint job, pitted, lumpy. From Quebec's Eastern Townships region. "Orange-peeling" is a widespread term for what happens to a poor paint job, imperfectly baked on, etc.

organ transplant — rider of a motorcycle, from the point of view of a new-age child: "Look, there goes an organ transplant!"

orificer — deliberate mispronunciation of "officer," this is a cop who throws the book at you (said with a country accent).

O-rings — Remember the Challenger and her O-rings? Even a bend in a high pressure pipe, such as an airconditioner line, will cause pressures to become excessive, and O-ring failure can result.

orphan car — as name implies, a car no longer manufactured, or, as in Opel's case, no longer imported to these shores. Famous orphans: Triumph cars, DeLorean, Sunbeam Tiger. The rub? Parts for orphaned cars are expensive or are made of near-**unobtainium.** Usually orphan owners band together with newsletters, clubs, auto events, so that they can swap parts and lies about how great the cars are.

outbraking, latebraking — "a classic overtaking maneuver in which you brake later than your opponent going into a turn. It is also a great way to **kiss** a wall or **shunt**." —from CHB. In the famous 1954 Le Mans road race, Jaguar won because it outbraked the competition, with four-wheel disc brakes. It is said that at the end of the Mursanne straight stretch, during the night portion of the 24-hour race, the brakes would glow cherry red with the heat of the friction.

out of sight guarantee — slightly better than standard "auction" guarantee (as is, where is), out-a-sight means exactly what it says. "Guaranteed to run good all the way out of sight of the used car lot." AKA **around the block guarantee.** Art Grindle, famous Dallas-Ft. Worth area Plymouth dealer, used to guarantee that his used cars would make it home if your home was in Dallas or Tarrant Counties. Art Grindle, God rest his soul, had "white sales" just like Sears does with bedsheets. He would appear on TV, sweating, waving his arms, "Folks, I've bought too many white cars" ...he would plead, "I'm selling them for $150 over invoice." (His clincher would be a followup such as..."I'll give you a hundred dollars trade-in for *any* car that'll *drive in to* my dealership." Folks fell for it, too. Bringing their beasts in, they left in white Plymouths, until the freeways would take on a pale white blur. (On the utility of a white car in Texas, see **black plate temperature.**)

outrun the note — used car term, for "a car that will run longer than the monthly payments". "Think it'll outrun the note?" See **note lot.**

out to pasture — cars, not cows. Artie has a bit of pasture land out near Elroy where he stores old cars, no longer running, but with lots of good parts left on them. Out to pasture is exactly that....a form of, well, life in suspension. Ever hear of the Cadillac Ranch up near Amarillo, Tex., ...ten Caddys stuck (buried) sticking up at an angle out of the dirt? A monument to the tail fin!

overpriced sewing machine — used to describe a Porsche in the early 1960s in the movie American Graffitti.

over-rev — to increase the speed of a motor to a dangerous degree. See **rev.**

Oversqueeze Motors — local name for Dallas' Overseas Motors.

overturned soup spoon — jocular description, based on the appearance of the design, of the early 1960s Porsche. See also **soap dish.**

Ovlov — Volvo.

Owner's Manual — Sounds obvious as hell, but the owner of a car is responsible for everything in the Owner's Manual. Read the fine print.

P

pace car — no car shall pass the pace car (source: SCCA rules.) Cars shall hold positions behind pace car.

pack — a convoy, bunch of speeding scofflaws. (It used to be said "you can't get out of Texas going 55 mph." The crossing time, from El Paso to Texarkana, was three days. Now it's "You can't get out of Texas going 65."

paint it candy apple red and race it — on explaining why she finally sold her favorite 1955 Chevrolet, one woman said "They swore they'd paint it candy apple red and race it!" (Famous lies of the twentieth century)

the **paint scraper** — the Lotus Esprit Turbo, because it looks like one.

pancaked — flattened, "as a hood that has been cut, a section removed, and rewelded but with less arch. Usually on pre-60s cars when hoods were more rounded." —from Paul Burrill, Madison WI. Also known as **decked.**

pan head — Harley Hog engine, valve cover is pan shaped. See also **flat head, knuckle head, shovel head, block head.**

panic stop — real hard, serious, skillful, careful application of brakes. In the Boy Scout Manual, you are told you're never supposed to panic. But what about when you — Honda 50cc motorcycle — have right of way, and it — Mack truck — runs stop sign? You —VW beetle — and it —Greyhound bus — have to share some space in the road?

paraffin — British term for "kerosene."

Paris-Dakar race — most godawful test of four wheel drive cars, offroad motorcycles, and trucks ever devised. 8000 mph at 120 mph, mostly desert, and bad, bad lands. Scorpions, sneak thieves. Legal robbery when contestants purchase supplies, gasoline, etc.

put it in **park, pecker** — way to say "cool down, chill out," derived from car talk. —80s slang.

parking lot — crowded interstate highway when traffic, instead of doing 65 mph, slows to a crawl.

parts changer — a derogatory term for mechanic, suggesting that instead of understanding and fixing the problem, he simply replaces every questionable part, charging enormous sums for this service. See **grease monkey, shotgunning it.**

pass key — have you got the ....? (bolt cutters)

patch out — **peel out, burn off**.

Pathfinder — one of several "smart car" systems to provide navigation and control assistance to help make traffic flow better in congested areas. "Completed in 1991 at a cost of $11.9 million, this was an attempt to speed traffic along a stretch of the Santa Monica Freeway in California. Road-imbedded sensors monitored traffic and TV cameras spotted accidents; this information was used to manipulate traffic lights. GM provided 25 cars with computer navigation systems so their drivers could tap into alternate route suggestions from the control centre." —Timothy Pritchard, "Smart Cars down the road," Toronto *Globe and Mail* (February 1, 1993). See also **Prometheus, Drive, TravTek.**

pavement puppy — drivers that are continuously off of the **racing line**, the line around the race track, through the corners, etc., that represents the shortest course given speed and centrifugal force.

paycheck car — a used car that may be purchased with one paycheck, used until it breaks, then junked.

peaky — machine that develops peak horsepower in a narrow rpm band, making it extremely hard to control. **Squirrelly. Cammy. Coming on the cam.** The opposite of **low-end grunt.**

pedal to the metal — holding the car at its top possible speed.

peel out, peel (Nova Scotia), **peel away, peel it** — see **burn off, lay rubber.**

penguins — a Southern California term for the little reflectors set into American freeways to mark the lanes, this one from their yellow in the middle, white on edges. Also known as **Botts dots, city titties, drunk bumps, cat's eyes.** See also **reading Braille.**

people eater — highly modified, fast racing motorcycle, specifically designed for its purpose and *no one but its owner/driver has any business on it.* I. e. Steve Brown's BMW Turbo R90S.

peppy — trade buzz word for a tiny motor which has to turn 7000 rpm just to go down the road at 60 mph.

percolate — run well, move right along smoothly, said of a car or motor. The word also describes the dynamic of fuel vaporization in hot weather.

persuade — jocular diminutive description of what happens when you have to hammer something. "Yes, it was seized right up, but I persuaded it." See **Harley tuning wrench.**

persuader — any large tool used for applying excessive force, e. g. hammer (3 lb. and up), prybar, cheater, large vise-grips, etc. "You're not using enough persuasion there, Jack."

petrol — British term for gasoline (from "petroleum") See also **benzine, benzina, ethyl.**

piano tops — pistons with "pop-up", raised layer in the top, to increase compression, the shape of the raised section corresponding roughly to that of a Steinway piano seen from above.

they're taking **pictures on the Pershing** — cabbie radio talk in Austin, upon seeing a radar trap on the Pershing parkway from airport into town.

picking daisies — careening wildly off the road. Also known as **mowing the lawn.**

pickle chaser — CB radio slang for a hooker who calls up lonely truckers (usually on Channel 19) and suggests that they switch channels to, say, Channel 15 or 16.....to "talk" about a "date."

pickled — in its own juices. For various reasons, when doing a valve job, for instance, one must remove a car's radiator and store it for two weeks (while the head is in the machine shop). The radiator is left with coolant in it, hoses attached to it, plugged up, etc., so that it doesn't dry out and form deposits/scale etc. in its innards. Same goes for fuel pumps.

pig — see **minoune, boat, land yacht......**

Pillage BMW — local name for "Village BMW," Austin TX, now defunct.

pimpmobile — a large, flashy car, in Halifax a Lincoln or big Ford with dark windows and a telephone. In Montreal, a stretch Cadillac limousine, white or gold.

pinché — in the phrase "this pinché truck," this typical Mexican curse means "cheap."

ping — the awkward and unsettling engine noise, "valves, probably", you tell yourself, caused by low octane fuel or faulty timing. Known in England as "pinking."

Pininfarina — Italian bodymaker, designer, perhaps the most famous. Designed the Alfa convertibles, BMW 2002, Peugeot 304, etc.

pinking — British term for **ping**. See **knock.**

pink slip — old expression for "car title" ("Let's race for pink slips!"). A different meaning from "what you get when you get fired."

Pinto — Portuguese slang for "small male organ." —from Maggie Maier's "Wow, a sporty, five-speed matron," in Toronto *Globe and Mail*, March 3, 1992.

coming on the **pipe** — also known as **getting on the pipe, putting on the pipe.** Accelerating a powerful engine (e. g. a Porsche) into the power band, causing the sound to come up smoothly and, to the ear of a person who loves cars, beautifully. (The pipe is the tailpipe, and the accent in this phrase is on the *sound*.) Don Hackett has pointed out that it is the tuned exhaust that makes the sound, when it reaches the resonant frequency; it has a performance dimension, a too, as the tuned pipes extract the waste gases rapidly and efficiently. A British way to say this is **coming on song,** coming on the **mega.**

piss bike — a little runty bike without enough power to "pull the slack out of the chain."

pissing on a spark plug — has both figurative and literal meanings.
Figurative: to put oneself at person, even intimate bodily risk to get the job done, even knowing the consequences.
Literal: bearing this in mind, old-fashioned cars had no rubber insulating boots on their spark plugs.

is that **piss yellow or lemon yellow?** — he bellows out of the win-

dow as the two cars pull alongside each other on the "strip."
"It's **piss** yellow," the other yells back, grinning.
The idea is a lemon yellow car isn't as good a machine as a piss yellow one. —from the movie American Graffiti.

piston slap — not just a **knock**, but a *loud* knock, a sure sign of a worn-out cylinder. Usually a mystery sound caused by a very loose or galled piston. Discernable from other engine sounds by two characteristics: isn't heard at all rpms and has a "double knock" to it.

pit cupcake — Female "'friends' of the drivers and pit crew. See: Scoring Championship Points." —from C. H. B. in the San Antonio *Current* the day before the San Antonio Gran Prix (1988). Also known as "pit puppy."

pit racing — illegal and dangerous stuff. Friends, even children of racers, driving their cars/bikes/minibikes fast in the pit area of a racetrack.

pit wall — important wall separating the pits from the mechanics.

pit wolfie — or "pit groupie," an attractive buxom young woman, usually scantily clad.....a pit crew member with nominal function. "They also serve who only stand and wait."

plain jane — ordinary, usually big comfortable, souped-up, unmarked highway patrol car. Sometimes not so big—see **cop 'stang.**

planetary gears — gears designed and fitted together to work in coordination, three or more rotating outside one at the center, all within an inner-geared moving housing , to achieve slower or higher speed and torque increase or decrease. A component of automatic transmissions.

plastic Jesus — favorite of Latin population, on **taco wagons.** "I don't care if it rains or freezes, long as I got my plastic Jesus, taped on to the dashboard of my car......" Some of them glow in the dark!

un **Poche —** satirical deliberate mispronunciation, in Quebec French, of "Porsche." Literally means "a pocket," but in slang, "a scrotum", or "the bulge in the crotch."

pocket rocket — the first small Oldsmobile, the **gutless Cutlass,**

1973-74, with four cylinders. The company called it the F85. — a joint, doobie, "reefer."

pollution control devices — new automotive features of the 1980s: the **smog pump**, which pumps air into hot exhaust gases, further reburning them (see "to go **Nova**"); the **gulp valve,** which feeds air to exhaust from the smog pump; **E. G. R**. ("exhaust gas recirculation"), which is a valve mechanism that does, in small amounts, what it says it does and helps prevent icing.

ponies — horsepower (term commonly used by bike racers).

Pontiac — **P**oor **O**ld **N**egro **T**hinks **I**t's **A C**adillac.

pookey — sticky stuff (anti-squeak compound) applied to back of brake pads.

Popemobile — modified (bulletproof) Lincoln Continental. See also **President's car.**

poppin Johnnie — the old John Deere opposed twin tractor, so called because the opposed twin fired both cylinders simultaneously, generating lots of pulling (plowing) torque. You could hear a poppin' Johnnie several miles away in West Texas, when we were kids.

Dr. Ferdinand **Porsche** — famous gifted designer, of the cars bearing his name, and also of the original VW.

Porsche baiter — the Mazda RX-7, such a hot little sports car that it has to have a special steering and suspension damper. See **sport mode, economy mode.**

Porsche driver — "always first at the scene of the crash."

portholes — row of chromed fake exhausts along edges of hood of a 1949 Buick Roadmaster. The manufacturer's name for them was "Cruisaline Ventaports."

positrac — positraction, the General Motors name for its limited-slip differential.

potato chipping — brake defect. See **runout.**

power band — where engine develops power, usually at 2500-4500 rpm in V8s, 3500-5500 in foreign cars.

power brake and jet off-take — attributes of a 1973 Buick Electra that Ace, famous local black used-car salesman in Austin, Texas, was extolling to another soul brother.

power envelope — engineering visual or graphic term for the shape that shows how quickly a source of power builds after the acceleration is applied as well as how long it lasts after it is taken off. The gasoline power envelope is quick to grow, but falls off immediately; the steam power envelope built a little more slowly but lasted much longer. "The main reason gas replaced steam was the need to fill up with water every hundred miles."

power run — fun rally or enduro event where entrants, as they ride, pick up five or seven playing cards, one per check point (usually), and, at end of run, best entrant's hand wins prize/trophy.

power shift — in drag racing, to keep the throttle depressed all the way through each shift, thus allowing the motor to build **revs** and torque. Gets impressive **rubber.** This one, I guarantee, will burn your clutch up, fast.

pranged — dented, "dinged," caused minor damage. British term, but also in use in Newfoundland, and then in Cape Breton, Nova Scotia. "Pranged her in the parking lot last night, did you?" "Pranged" originally came from the British Royal Air Force, where it meant "a crash." A "wizard prang" was a total write-off.
The authors of this book are of the opinion that the "prang" illustration in John Lawlor's *How to talk car* is actually an instance of **T-boning.**

pregnant roller skate — small imported sports car, especially the VW Beetle. See also **cheese covered roller skate.**

presidential quality — said of an airconditioning system that blows whisper quiet and cold, so cold "it'll give you arthritis."

President's car — modified (bulletproof) Lincoln Continental. John Kennedy was the last President to ride in an open car.

pressed ham — winter version of the **moon,** done with the window rolled up.

"Slow down," Dad exclaims, "I'm about to **press my foot through the floorboard."** — something Dads do whenever their sons are driving. (Imaginary/wishful? braking involuntary reaction)

Dad's driving— a series of quick jabs on brake pedal, quick glances at imagined/real obstacles. They oughta be outlawed.

Prince of Darkness — always means only one man, Joseph Lucas, from the world of automotive electronics, the British electrical equipment manufacturer, famous for the Lucas headlight systems, which are notoriously unreliable. The company's slogan, for mechanics and people who know, is unconsciously funny: "Don't go out at night." It has been said that the reason the British like warm beer is that beer is often kept in Lucas refrigerators. In the U. K., he's known as the **Inventor of Night.**

prndl — Park, Reverse, Neutral, Drive, Low — automatic transmission! Pronounced "pernundull".

probe — a big pry bar, in jocular diminutive. "It was hard to get in there. Had to use the probe!"

Prometheus — one of several "smart car" systems designed to provide navigation and control assistance to help move traffic in congested areas. Stands for "Program for European Traffic With Highest Efficiency and Unprecedented Safety." "An eight-year (1986-1994), $800-million effort to develop onboard technologies for collision avoidance and navigation....Including large European car makers and suppliers, governments, etc., includes vision enhancement for night or fog condition driving with infrared cameras sensing heat from objects within 30 metres and creating a road picture, intelligent cruise control, using microwave radar, maintaining speed and distance with cars ahead by manipulating brakes and throttle." —Timothy Pritchard, "Smart Cars down the road," Toronto *Globe and Mail* (February 1, 1993). See also **Pathfinder, Drive, TravTek.**

pro-street — "narrowing the rear differential so wider tires can be installed, all within the fenders. Tires can be as wide as 32"." —from Paul Burrill, Madison WI.

protest — in order to protest another competitor's engine, to reveal and discredit a cheater, one puts in a request form and puts up a sum of money equivalent to the cost of "teardown" of motor ("protest money"). Refundable, if protested engine is revealed to be illegally modified, i. e. **bored and stroked,** revealed by measurement.

prototype — one of a kind car, or experimental model. —from CHB.

Prussian blue — name of a color known in England as **Engineer's blue.** The blue powder used to uncover mechanical imperfections in metal surfaces, which tests and reveals the fit of gear faces, etc., is the source of this term.

prying it loose from his cold, dead fingers — "You can have my (gun, motorcycle, etc.) just as soon as you pry my cold, dead fingers off of it."

Doug walked across the neatly manicured lawn....up the three steps to the door....the correct initials were woven into the aluminum screen door...."Does a Colonel Jas. Sanders live here?" Doug asked the elderly, plump lady who answered his knock.

"Why, yes," she replied, "he's taking the sun back in the dining room....Come on in."

Looking lifeless, the frail, dried up little stick of a man was reclined in a wheel chair, a blanket over him, with the sun shining on his legs.

"Oh, Colonel," she says, "a man is here to see you...."

He wakes up.

"Ahem," Doug begins, "I understand that you have an old Indian 'Chief' motorcycle."

"Best damn motorcycle ever built," the old bird snaps, regaining a bit of his faded military bearing. "Ethel, roll me into the garage."

It was sitting in the middle of the garage floor, leaning heavily on its sidestand....The old 74-cubic inch V-twin Chief was covered in dust....its leather saddlebags heavily rhinestoned...cracked and dusty....Like a dust-covered time machine, ready, somehow, to time travel.

"Those new bikes aren't as fast as this," the colonel says, his voice a little stronger now. "Hell, Ethel and I went all around the South on this, years ago. I'd kill her if she ever sold it while I was in the hospital." He coughs.

"It's beautiful," Doug murmurs, holding back his next question.

Leaving, Doug hands his card to Ethel at the front door. "Ma'am," he says quietly, "if...the situation ever arises....where you don't know what to do with that...er...machine in your garage....please call me....." And, glancing over her shoulder, to make sure they weren't being observed, she takes his card.

psych out — to intimidate other drivers/ competitors. People do various things: on the starting line/ at the red light, **revving it up** and almost letting the clutch out several times.....the vehicle jumps convincingly...You can be ticketed for this in many small towns, but not in Mexico City.

pucker factor — "guts, courage, or recklessness depending on your point of view." —from C. H. B. in the San Antonio *Current* the day before the San Antonio Gran Prix (1988). Originally from airplane talk: the centrifugal force applied to the face when pulling out of a dive says it all. ("The pucker occurs at the other end of the anatomy" — anon. Brit.)

pucks — early slang name for brake pads, which in some cases were round.

puddin' skins — slick tires. See also **banana peels.**

puddlejumper — old jocular affectionate term for a car, from the 1930s in West Texas.

puffing the blues — expression from British Columbia, Canada, for what a car does when it burns oil. The smoke is blue.

pull — to remove a part from a car, for inspection, repair, or replacement.

won't **pull the slack out of the chain** — said of a motorcycle with very little power, because of lack of compression or poor tuning etc.

pumpkin — "the pumpkin" in mechanics' talk is the cover for the differential, because of its shape. "Center section of the rear differential": —from Paul Burrill, Madison WI.

Punch Buggy — a game popular among teenagers of the 1980s in Toronto. First person to spot a VW Beetle says "punch buggy red" (or whatever, naming the color of the car), and thus gets the right to punch the other person hard on the upper arm.

While cars are supposed to provide major excitement in twentieth century life, they are the source of many such games which suggest that some passengers find riding in them boring. There's "points for peds," in which the driver tallies points for running over various pedestrians pointed out by passengers—5 pts. for a boy, 20 for a girl and boy together, 50 bonus for an old lady, 100 for a mother and child—all verbally, of course. Other games involve counting the number of cars of a certain color, trying to be the first to name the car type and year, "pediddle"—in which you try to be the first to notice a car with one headlight burned out, etc.

punt — As in football, sometimes all you can do. "When it's fourth and long, fall back and punt." ("Ma'am," he says, "that knocking sound your car is making means the rod bearings are gone, and the smoke coming out the back means the rings are gone, and the flame means it's on fire. I'll pay you twenty dollars to drive it away.")

push — to follow someone very close on the freeway, clearly encouraging him/her to pull over and let you pass.

— "if a driver turns the wheel but not enough steering results, the car is said to have too much **push**, also known as understeer." —from CHB. "The driver enters a corner and when he turns the steering wheel the front end of the car shows a slight reticence to follow that direction, tending to 'push' its way toward the outside of the race track." —"Riding a New Wave," *Eagle Performance Report* (Spring 1991).

push, pull, or drag sale — car dealer's come-on sign to suggest you may bring any vehicle for a trade-in and get a deal on the purchase of a car. Universal in North America: a classic practitioner of this kind of sale was Terry Balcan in Winnipeg, Manitoba.

put a potato in the exhaust pipe — deliberate subtle sabotage of an automobile by someone in a cold rage.

Q–R

Q-ship — journalistic nickname for Infinity Q-45 (by Nissan), named for infamous disguised "killer" ships of WW II (German). Why? is an appropriate question, because Q-45 is fast, but not that fast. Sound system is considered "killer" by younger set.

race cars with names — "Grounds for Divorce" is a shiny white Camaro, jacked up in rear slightly, fat tires, and loud and fast.
"No Checks - Cash Only" is a beaten up brown-on-blue monster from wrecking yard sponsor. Loud, fast, handling questionable, wobbles on hard braking.
My money is on "Grounds."
—research at Austin Speed-o-rama, 10 miles or so south of town on Hwy 183, Friday night's race. See also **roundy round.**

race face — sorta like boxer's cold stare just before the event, a look of utter seriousness. —from Bruce Brown's documentary film "On Any Sunday II".

racer chaser — see **pit cupcake** — from C. H. B. in the San Antonio *Current* the day before the San Antonio Gran Prix (1988).

racing line — the imaginary line around a race track, as close to the inside as is consistent with speeds and centrifugal force, which represents the best and fastest possible course during the race. Richard Sommer, a Buddhist from Quebec and a teacher of Robert Persig's *The Zen of Motorcycle Maintenance*, says there's a mystical dimension to the racing line, because it is not a straight line, but elliptical.
Stirling Moss has said that a great racing car driver has "proprioception," the power to know through an inner perception where he is in space, and has compared driving well to ballet dancing. —in Denis Jenkinson's *The Racing Driver*.

racing luck — bad luck, strongly akin to Murphy's Law ("if anything can go wrong, it will"). From Howard Hawks' movie "Red Line 7000."

racing slicks — tires made with no treat, to give better traction where the rubber meets the road. Also known as **slicks.**

radical cam — a camshaft designed for high rough idle, set so both intake and exhaust are generous, to dump lots of fuel through the system when it's opened up, giving lots of power. The reason why high-performance cars go "rump, rump, rump" with a deep throaty sound, at stop lights, sounding as if they're about to die. Also known as "full race cam" and "three-quarter race cam," depending on degree of "lift" (how open it makes the valve) and "dwell," (how long it makes it open).

radio — in "you can't outrun the radio," the word refers to the police radio which may be used to signal ahead and make sure a speeder gets busted even though he can outrun the cop who first spotted him.

ragadoon — a particularly ugly used car, usually parked in the back row of the used car lot.

rag top — convertible. The word comes from the days before "hardtop" convertibles, when they were really convertible, with a cumbersome set of winches and a canvas covering which folded back and let the sun and wind show you off.

rail job — dragster in which the body is mainly reduced to very strong chassis (frame).

rake — "angle of the car, usually the rear higher than the front." —from Paul Burrill, Madison WI.

Rambler — now extinct, this American Motors car lives on in car talk by being used to designate any car that is obsolete when built. It did have certain advantages that made it popular; for example, teenagers really liked the fact that the front seats would fold right down.

rat — a big-block Chevrolet, as contrasted with a **mouse.** —from Erwin Schieder.

rat bike — bike afflicted/adorned with patched stuff, baling wired fenders, faded and scratched paint, but running.

rat fink — "Big Daddy" Ed Roth's large-eared mouse character, cartooned in drag racing magazines in 1960s-70s. Ed Roth, world famous California car customizer extraordinaire, built loads of wild dragster-style street rods.

rats leaving a sinking ship — cars leaving the workplace en masse.

Rat Trap — "A police anti-theft car, known as the Rat Trap, was stolen from Bath Lane, Newcastle upon Tyne, England. The engine of the white E-registered Ford Sierra, which has caught 31 thieves in the past 18 months, should have died after only 20 yards and hidden door and window locks trapped the thieves inside. A police spokesman said, 'There was a malfunction.'" —London *Observer* (11 October 1992), p. 2.

rattle patrol — "Well," he said, "I'll jack her up and go on 'rattle patrol,' and mebbe derattleify her." Mechanic's term for process of finding and fixing rattles.

raw eyes — opinion from an unofficial or unprofessional viewpoint.

RCH — a term of rough measure, as in "set the points at 15/1000ths, plus or minus an RCH." The letters stand for "red cunt hair," and there's a finer unit than that: TRCH (a "titch" of an RCH). This unit of measurement is also used in carpentry.

rear view mirror — "whats-a behind me is not-a important" — Italian sports car drivers say as they rip off their rear view mirrors and toss them.

reading Braille — wandering into the **drunk bumps.** See **city titties.**

recall — factory letter comes out....you open it.....and read "The brakes in your pickup truck may fail at any moment." Horrified, you watch your spouse approach, turn into driveway, and try to brake.....Truck smashes into back of your car. Recalls......lawyers.....think about it.......Lawyers need work.

red handle — fire extinguisher handle in place next to the shift lever in a race car, to release fire extinguisher chemical from f. e. already in place under the hood.

those little **red rags** — "I don't use those little red rags," Artie says, speaking from beneath a car. "They cost a quarter each....I get a whole *bag* of rags from the Goodwill for a buck." (A commotion begins...) "Quick," he says, "hand me a clean rag...something's dripping onto my face....." (Stepping over to the rag bag, I select a very large black pair of women's panties and place them in his hand, stretching out from under the car. Pulling them in, Artie mops his face, and then gags violently, raising up involuntarily. He strikes his head on the bottom of the car. His face appears from beneath the car. "God," he says, still spitting, "don't you know that they don't wash these things!"

never buy a **red used car** — on the theory and experience that people who buy red cars tend to be the same people who like to drive their cars fast, push them hard, wear them out. The same rule, for the same reason, applies to the GM Firebird and the Toyota Celica, according to Robert Appel, in *The Used Car Believer's Handbook.* It is interesting to note that in Japan, red cars are outlawed for ordinary citizens, being reserved for fire and rescue vehicles only. In America, on the other hand, polls show that 57% of the citizenry *like red cars.* In Canada, blackflies prefer blue to red..... —from Judith Ritter, CBC Home Run, 18 January 1990, reporting on the Montréal Auto Show.

ree-raw — to abrade severely (flesh, tires, etc.). "Boy, that 50 mph slide on my backside ree-rawed my leathers *and* my ass."

remodel — slang bodyshop term for "destroyed", as in "I see you remodeled your front end." Borrowed from carpentry? where the onset of a remodel job resembles a bomb explosion.

Renault "Encore" — An international car, French design, brakes made in Canada, wheel bearings in Brazil, electrics in Mexico, and **ass-sembled** in USA (with both metric and English sized bolts and nuts).

Reo — This name, seen mainly on trucks and buses, was derived from the name of a builder of automobiles, R. E. Olds. During the 1930s, as the many gave way to the few with the emergence of the Big Three (Ford, General Motors, Dodge-Chrysler-AMC), R. E. Olds was bought out by GM, the deal being that he'd have responsibility for one of their better cars, the Oldsmobile, with his own name being retained in the form "Reo" for trucks and buses. "I remember a fleet of Reo Speedwagons — immaculate in Red Cab, Green Body, owned by a furniture removal company in U. K. in 1943/4. The removal van was called a 'pantechnicon!'" —anon. Brit.

replicar — see **kit car.**

repo man — specialist in stealing cars from people who haven't made the payments, on fee from the mortgage holder. The repo man did not ring the doorbell and say "I've come to take your car." He hooked it up to a wrecker and took it away, as quickly as possible, and in broad daylight, midday. Subject of a hilarious movie by the title "Repo Man." In recession-plagued Texas in the mid-eighties, "repo resale" lots are a sign of the times on highways between San Antonio and Dallas.

retro-fit — improved part designed to be used as replacement in older models, so as to improve safety, performance, etc. E. g. nylon alternator bushings for BMW automobiles to replace rubber ones which melt in the heat in extreme climates (like Texas).

rev — to speed up a motor, increasing its "revs" or "revolutions per minute." See also **over-revving.**

reversed, to reverse — drove, to drive, in reverse gear (British car talk)

reverse gear — in the Model-T, when a hill was too steep to climb using the torque developed by the early motors in forward gears, you could often get up by turning the car around and backing up it, because reverse was the largest gear wheel, and had more torque.

reverse gear holeshot — I did it with a Rolls-Royce "Shadow" behind me. I didn't hit him, but you should have seen the look on his face when my Volvo lurched back his way. Incredibly enough it happens at the drag races now and then, with disastrous results. With quick shift gearbox linkage in the heat of competition, the driver will actually get the thing in reverse and rev it up and pop the clutch.....

reverse gear horn — goes beep....beep....beep as big dump truck goes backwards. Mandatory equipment on city work machines. Fitted as standard feature on some Volvo heavy-duty construction vehicles.

riceburners — Japanese cars. Also **fishheads, sushimobiles, Jap scrap.** Not often heard since the early days of Japanese cars in the U. S., as the reliability of these cars is widely known.

a ride — a motorcycle. "What's your ride?"

ride — "getting a team to let you drive a car in the race." —from C. H. B. in the San Antonio *Current* the day before the San Antonio Gran Prix (1988).

ride the rings off her — racers with underpowered machines sometimes push the engine until it smokes. The rings can't "come off," just wear out. To run it until exhaust smoke fogs the track so bad the officials **black flag** you. See **road fogger.**

riding bitch — especially in a pickup, riding in the middle of the seat. The term comes from the convention that the driver's girlfriend rides next to him, and his friend **rides shotgun** on the right-hand side.

riding Indian style — men in the front seat, women in the back.

riding shotgun — especially in a pickup, riding on the right-hand side next to the window. See also **riding bitch.**

ring-ding — slang term for a two-stroke engine, because of its sound, a noisy shake and rattle. Also known as **whiz-bang,** and **rock in a tin can.**

ringer — "a car that does not pass **scrutineering**".

ring job — new piston rings "to get better sealing around the pistons." — Robert Appel, *The Used Car Believer's Handbook.*

roach coach — pickup truck with coffee, sandwiches, snacks, a catering truck, which comes around construction sites and garages at break-time. Also known as the **maggot wagon.**

roadfogger — a car that emits a lot of smoke from the exhaust, e. g. an old BMW with worn rings. See also **oilburner.**

road kill — dead animals found on the roads after they were hit by cars. Gary Snyder recommends investigating their possibilities as food in crisis; for another use, see George Heyduke's *Get Even* (Paladin Press).

road map — drawing or sketch of layout of hoses, etc. that must be removed to service a vehicle.

road rage — she **shitting contest.**

road rash — abraded skin, like **gravel rash.** See also **beef it.**

road signs — how Andice, Texas got named. On I-35 between Austin and Dallas, originally a wide spot in the road, with a beer store. The sign, "Beer and Ice", cracked during a norther, and the "beer" part of the sign blew down. "Andice" was left. Folks liked the name, and that was it.

roadster — a particular kind of sports car, a convertible (i. e. no fixed top) with very flimsy top and windows. The windshield was small; the side windows did not roll up and were often of canvas and isinglass rather than glass, "side curtains." Examples include most British sports cars of the 1950s and 60s, especially the MG TC, TD, and TF, and the Porsche Speedster.
The term was also used to designate a specific Indy 500 race car, built by Kurtis, which was lower and wider than most because the engine was on its side and the drive shaft passed beside, not under the driver. See also **runabout.**

"In my view your examples are 'sports cars.' A Roadster is halfway betwen a sports car and an 'open tourer' (convertible) — it's a 'sporty car.'" —anon. Brit.

road test — this ordinary technical term from mechanic shops gets jocular use to mean "to toss out of vehicle with intent to destroy" as for example, a stereo system or radio, to watch it bounce.

Roadway — Roadway Trucking Lines, with many trucks on America's freeways. Always on the road, always in the way.

Robin Phucker — stunt word mythical name of the service manager of the local (competitor) BMW dealership, as applied by the freelance BMW mechanic with his own shop. "Yes, ma'am, take it over to Whatsisnames and ask for Robin Phucker!"
rock crusher — manual 4-speed transmission, heavy duty and overbuilt, from the very loud metallic sound it makes, increasing the possibility of **grinding the gears,** on the Muncie model M-22 Corvette.

Rocket sled on wheels — dream car, from ZZTop's album Tush.

Roger Penske — famous Formula I road racer, now known as founder of Penske Racing (winner in 1988 Indianapolis 500).

Roll-A-Maze — it was nothing, absolutely nothing more than a wooden box, an open wooden box one foot square, with a perforated masonite platform suspended in its center. The platform tilts.....controllable by two 90 degree-opposed wooden knobs. The object of the game is to direct...roll...a steel ball bearing from 1 to 49, avoiding all of the holes the ball may/will/can fall into. It's hard to control the little steel ball.

"If you can do this," Steve was saying, jiggling the little ball to the next spot, "you can balance the carbs on a Jaguar, and they say they'll hire you over at the sports car repair shop!"

rolled and pleated — 1950s car interior styling, still commonly done in Mexican (border) upholstering shops, whether you want it or not.

roller — a Rolls-Royce. Also **Rolls.** "When Lowell Thomas asked T. E. Lawrence (of Arabia) just after the first World War if there was anything he couldn't afford but would like to have, he said, 'I should like to have a Rolls-Royce car with enough tyres and petrol to last me all my life.' He never got his wish." —Fox and Smith, *Rolls-Royce: The Complete Works.*

rolling chicane — Mr. and Mrs. Borogove, mimsying...... see **herd it down the road.**

rolling stop — putting on the brakes as you approach the stop sign, but not coming to the kind of complete, full stop called for by the law and observed during driving license examinations. The term is an oxymoron, a contradiction in terms. Around the West Island of Montréal, known as a "Hudson rolling stop," because in the town of Hudson, Quebec, along the main approach road to the village, there's a stop sign in the middle of a straight stretch which doesn't have **speed bumps.** It is intended to slow down traffic. But local residents—especially attractive women in white convertibles—routinely observe it with a classic "rolling stop."

Also known as a **New York stop, California rolling stop, Quebec stop, taxi stop, American stop.**

Rolls — short for Rolls-Royce. According to Mike Fox' and Steve Smith's *Rolls-Royce, The Complete Works: The Best 599 Stories about the World's Best Car* (London: Faber and Faber, 1984), "Rolls-Royces do not break down; they *fail to proceed.* " A story not in the book has it that a Rolls owner broke an axle in the African desert, and, after cabling the company, did not wait long—two mechanics were flown with new axle to the site to repair and get him on his way again. He waited, then, for the bill, and when it didn't come, contacted them again, only to be told: "There is no mistake, sir; Rolls Royce axles do not break!" (story from Pat Atwood, a variant on one *in* the book, thus suggesting that Rolls Royce has entered Folklore))

But, if the cars are amazing, the company isn't perfect: the name of the Silver Mist model was unintentionally funny in Germany, since "miszt" in German carries commonly the sense of "mists" as in "pisses," with a frequent pun on "missing" the urinal in men's rooms: "Mann irrt, wen er miszt." ("Man errs, when he misses, i. e. mists, i. e. pisses").

Rolls Rice — an apt term, considering the price of top of the line Japanese cars, for Nissan Maxima, Toyota Cressida, Acura Legend, etc. "What are you driving nowadays?" "Why....my Rolls Rice....of course." —with help from Catherine Chase. See also **riceburner.**

roll steering — how a sports car behaves, i. e. *steers* under hard cornering. Anti-sway bars come in various thicknesses, and are adjustable for **understeer** and **oversteer.**

romancing the engine — painting up and pinstriping it. Vette people did it a lot.

roo bar — **cow catcher** of Australian manufacture. Thicker, bigger, and stronger than the US equivalent — built to stop a *kangaroo.* (I personally saw one the other day on a Toyota Landcruiser.)

roostertail — plume or spray pattern of mud, water, rocks, etc. thrown up by spinning car wheels, especially when drifting corners in racing. You get them in heavy rain without any wheelspin. The "roost" is the upward-arcing stream of mud from a dirt-bike.

rope shocks — on cars with worn-out shock absorbers, **shade-tree mechanics** would sometimes simply attach a rope between the shock mounts. This device would not provide shock absorption, but it would limit the downward travel of the suspension, thus reducing the worst effects of the lack of proper equipment.

rotate/revolve — to **spin out.**

round de round — race track 1/8 to 1/4 mile oval, either dirt track or paved. Lots of noise, dust, smoke, action (such as sideswiping, crashes of various sorts — no headons). Research: Austin Speed-o-rama.

roundel — any circular identifying device, e. g. the blue and white BMW symbol, supposed to represent a spinning airplane propeller. BMW built the engine for the Foch-Wulf German fighter plane during World War II (Mercedes powered the Messerschmidt).

Returned fighter pilot, describing aerial combat for a mixed audience after the war: "And I looked up, and there was one fokker to the left, and one fokker to the right....."

Woman host breaks in...."I must explain that the 'Fokker' was a type of German fighter plane!"

Fighter pilot: "No, no, these fokkers was flying Messerschmidts!"

R & R — seen on your car's repair bill, means the opposite of "rest and relaxation"—"remove and replace" (e. g. dashboard, driveshaft, intake, etc.)

rubber — tires. "This car's got good rubber." See also **burning rubber.**

where the **rubber meets the road** — advertising slogan for tires. Ever notice those skid marks on the road that look as if the car was going backwards? The "hysterisis" factor in physics explains that as the tires **break loose,** the rubber's compressed, stored energy springs back in the other direction and makes those curious reversed skid marks.

rubbing block — little fibre block on ignition points that rides on distributor points cam. Do it yourselfers note: needs a drop of grease when points are replaced.

rubbing money on it — to fix it. This is an era of specialization, especially in car repair. Take your beastie to someone who specializes in (i. e. is familiar with) that type of car, or you're just **rubbing money on it.**

rubbing rails — the phrase for the wooden, rubber, or rope trim on boats which keep them from being scuffed up when they are tied to a wharf, this set of words from sea talk was adapted for car talk by Angus Walters, the legendary skipper of the Bluenose, Nova Scotia fishing schooner. He bought his first car, as the story goes, and drove it downtown. When he came to park it for the first time, he simply laid it up against the building at the side of the street, tearing off the chrome strip of trim. He drove it back to the dealer and asked for another one, explaining, "When I came to dock her downtown, she lost her wubbing wails!" (Walters was from Lunenburg County, where the German linguistic heritage of the people produces an odd pronunciation of "w"s and "r"s).

rumble seat — small rear seat in early cars, set in where the trunk is now. In U. K. — "dickey."

rumble strips — "a series of grooves in the road that hum and vibrate as you drive over them...[making a] pleasant middle-C hum, accompanied by a tingling and a gentle sense that you are accelerating,....[to make drivers slow down] at approaches to stop signs,..... [or on freeways] to bring sleepy drivers back to consciousness before they veer off the road." —Janet Torge, "Traffic Watch," in Montréal *Gazette*, January 8 1990. In use in Ohio for nearly twenty years. Their appeal to northern climates is that unlike **speed bumps** (U. S. South) or **sleeping policemen** (Mexico, Central America), they do not interfere with the operation of snowplows. Also known as **zip strips.** See also **drunk bumps, Botts dots, city titties, reading Braille.**
If they are at right angles, and you're on a bike, O. K.; if they are in line with the 'line of flight,' yikes.

runabout — an early name for a **roadster.**

running on the fumes or **running on empty** — to continue to drive even after the gas gauge shows the fuel tank is almost empty. Hence, in general use, a piece of car talk used to mean "burning the candle at both ends," driving oneself hard.

running the bike — in motorcycle racing, riders must sometimes climb hills so steep and/or slippery that the bike will not carry them up. They must dismount and, holding the handlebars and keeping the throttle open to the right acceleration, run beside the bike until they crest the hill. This manoeuvre is known as "running the bike."

runout — machinist's term, a measurement of the amount of warp in an automotive component. Such as a disc brake rotor, a disc which rotates in one plane.....theoretically warp, caused usually by heat, called **potato chipping.**

Russian dogsled — jocular term for a Lada.

Russian Fiat — the Yugo.

S

SAAB — Svenske Aeroplan Acti Belagit. For a clue to the meaning of the last two words, see **FIAT.**

Safety — first, always.

safety "twits" — NHTSA (National Highway Transportation and Safety Administration), according to Car and Driver magazine. Because they hate radar detectors and made Porsche, Ferrari, BMW, etc., put 85 mph maximum speedometers in cars that will do 170 mph. Nader's Raiders.

salad bar — an old car which looks rather nice in appearance but is rusted out completely in critical, hard-to-see areas, e. g. the frame. An automobile which is no longer safe to drive but which is still beautiful enough to wax and use as a salad bar. I saw this once in Vegas.

sandpapered — "the treatment" from new car dealership. They take your money, give you a car that doesn't perform properly, then they tell you you have to *wait* for it to be repaired...... "I've been sandpapered. This just chaps my ass." Another instance is having paid a five or six hundred dollar repair bill when you thought it was going to be $75. The reference to the ass is probably not accidental: that's where the wallet is. Steve Poteet used "chaps my ass" and "gravels my ass" interchangeably for this situation.

sand rail — dune buggy modification for loose sand—bigger tires, more ground clearance, snorkel for higher-off-ground air intake, etc. See **rail job.**

San Francisco sneaky — any one of a number of bizarre manoeuvres while behind the wheel in urban traffic. For example, a left-turn out of the far lane just as the light changes, when nobody else is there......

Satan's Choice — motorcycle gang in Quebec. See **Hell's Angels.**

savage rhythms — drums are well known to excite women's hips, get them dancing, etc. Harleys have those rhythms. My dumb new girlfriend, a coon ass she is, says "Low rumbly powerful engines have "em."

sawdust in the differential — like **bananas in the crankcase**, a British way to conceal the **knocking** that would give away to a potential purchaser serious internal damage to an engine highly likely to **eat its lunch.** "My Dad once bought a one-lunger bike with a wooden piston, and he was a good mechanic!" —Ken.

S belt — **Serpentine** belt system designed into some new cars (Ford). A great idea—only one flat, wide belt runs all accessories (power steering pump, alternator, airconditioning compressor, etc.), and it automatically tensions itself by a big spring-loaded pulley. Replaces multiple fan belt system. Self adjusting, doesn't slip. Advantages: one belt to adjust...more better safer. Why don't they do this on all cars?

scatter shield — stainless steel bell housing for clutch on dragsters. When irresistible force meets immovable object, something has got to give, and in the case of a drag race machine, that's usually the clutch....in the form of fragments blowing outward in every direction. Steel scatter shield is much stronger than cast iron stock parts.

Schadenfreude — German for "joy in (usually someone else's) pain." "Shameful joy." Actually enjoying someone else's misfortune. (Cruel German grins as he downshifts and passes slower, smoking British car....smiling and driving on past someone whose hood is up and smoke is billowing out.....) —from Helmut Barnett, who grew up in Stuttgart, next door to the original Porsche factory, which was originally in quonset huts and produced three cars a week.

"It had been raining all night in Tunisia and we had paused at the edge of a large, shallow, lakelike puddle on the coast road, to allow a moped driver to cross. Coming the other way, however, hove into view a speeding delivery truck.....a Peugeot, I think, its Arab driver grinning as he sped into the water, setting into motion a huge curling bow-wave (which engulfed the hapless moped and well-dressed driver), leaving the little machine drowned out, smoking, its driver soaked."

scofflaw — one who ignores traffic speed limits (especially the old 55 mph law), doesn't pay tickets, etc. Bad boys who drive **bad boy** cars. People with fast cars and radar detectors. People who bend the law. People who can't drive 65 mph.

scoops — air scoops, oversized air intakes built into the hood, facing forward, to let the carburetors take big gulps of air and drive it into the mix, to create or assist turbo effect. One of the best known was the Ram-Air on the GTO.

scoot — Hells Angels word for "motorcycle." "Lookit Tiny on his scoot!"

scope it out — a term which has passed into general use for "to figure it out," this probably originally derives from the word "oscilloscope," an electrical wave analyzer.

scoring championship points — "improving your standing in the various Camel GT series prize competitions. Or, garnering the admiration of **Pit Cupcakes**; or being the object of an attractive **Racer Chaser**; or, wearing your driving suit into a bar and flashing a gold card." —from C. H. B. in the San Antonio *Current* the day before the San Antonio Gran Prix (1988).

scrambles — European term for "motocross races."

screen test for the LAPD? —Subcategory: police car talk: suspect is handcuffed, put into back seat of cruiser but seat belt isn't fastened. Then cruiser is driven hard, with lots of sudden stops. Remember the screen between front and back seats? The screen test!

scrutineering — checking a (race) car to make sure it is legal.

seat belt — equipment to keep us in the car, forced on us by ambulance attendants so that they no longer have to prowl around looking for us after the accident.

seat belt interlock system override control button — Cars made in the seventies wouldn't start unless your seat belts were fastened. And sometimes, even *when* your belts were fastened, the car's "interlock system" still wouldn't let the thing start. So then, and by then the cars at the bank drive-thru are honking....you locate this button (usually *under the hood*, a brightly colored button mounted on a little box on the back firewall.) Don't you love advances in technology? Like **idiot-proofing** in *layers*. Anyhow, push button, get back in car, and start up.

seat of pants class — in enduro motorcycle racing, special "fun"class where timekeeping (with special MPH/chronometers/time charts, etc.) are not required. In fact, this class requires entrants *not* to have or rely on rally computers, clocks, or other instruments to run the rally with. This, of course, is for guys who want to run their motocross bikes, rather than play with gadgets.

sectioned — "a very difficult custom trick. A car is cut apart horizontally, several inches cut off, and then rewelded. The car usually looks lower and longer." —from Paul Burrill, Madison WI.

getting **seedy** — getting rusty.

Seek ye First the Kingdom of God Wrecking Yard — It is truly amazing the change that comes over these mean old farts who, stingy and tight all their lives, suddenly repent and paint Scripture all over the place when they realize that they are about to meet their Maker.

semi — a tractor-trailer rig, a big truck pulling a trailer. Also known as a **long-hauler.**

seven-klicker — Lucas Electric headlite switch on the TR7 [owners report replacing them several times a year. When the inevitable question is asked of the parts man — "How long is this switch guaranteed?" — Greg grins and says "seven klicks" (7 kilometres).

75OIL — easily misread as "75 OIL," this trim identification on the rear of the new V-12 BMW 750 series automobile should be read "750 IL". "I" means it has the fast camshaft, as opposed to "E", for "economy," and "L" means "luxury?" Probably. In Mercedes Benz 300SL and 300SLR, "Light", with "R" standing for "Rennsportswagen", "Racing Sports Car."

seven-window Chevy — pickup with split windshield, full back window, but two extra wraparound small windows at rear corners of cab; hence, seven-window Chevy!

sewing machine — the underpowered (1600 cc) little Ford products, such as Escort, Lynx, so that certain circuits have to shut down when others are operating, because there ain't enough juice to run everything at once.

shade-tree mechanic — an amateur fixer of cars, so called because he has no garage, and the tree in his yard is always surrounded by cars in various states of repair or deterioration. Many are being kept for parts. Freeland Reynolds Jr. of Nova Scotia says that a shade-tree mechanic's toolbox consists of a vi-segrip, a pipe wrench, and a broken screwdriver.

shake and bake sports sedan — fake sports car.

the **shape that wins** — a famous advertising slogan that either didn't work or backfired in some way. Coi-ned to announce British Leyland's new Triumph TR, referring to its "wedge shape," it became known to hardened British Leyland mecha-nics as "the shape that lo-ses/breaks/chokes."

shaved — "removing articles which protrude from the exterior of the car, such as door handles." —from Paul Burrill, Madison WI. See also **hid-den hinges.**

Sherwin-Williams overhaul — a jo-cular term for preparing a used car to resell without attempting to veri-fy or correct any mechanical pro-blems, but rather simply repainting it to make it look better.

shill — at an auto auction, a person paid by the dealership who owns the dog being auctioned, who bids on the thing against you, bidding the price up, then letting you bid last, thus getting their price. Strategy of the "shill" may backfire, and often does, in Austin. Shills are identified mainly by not being members of the "good old boys" cartel of used car guys, and bid against them, letting *them* get the winning bid.

shimmy — a wobble in the front wheels, usually discernible by a noticeable vibration in the stee-ring wheel. Caused by tire imba-lance, typically at speeds of 50-70 mph. Front wheel drive cars are specially sensitive to tire imba-lance.

The term comes from a dance named for its original perfor-mance by a dancer at an early twentieth century Worlds Fair (St. Louis or Chicago) who performed wearing only a man's shirt (from French "chemise.") See Lewis J. Poteet's *The South Shore Phrase Book* (Hantsport, N. S.: Lancelot Press, 1988).

keep the **shiny side up and the greasy side down** — trucker's slo-gan, also a pilots' oral rule.

shit and git — said of a 60's fast car, referring, of course, to the great cloud of exhaust, smog smo-ke, unburned gas, that rolls out, belches, from the exhaust of a big

V-8 when the throttle is opened up. Best example: the Shelby "AC" Cobra, with its huge 427 cubic inch engine.

shit-box — the Chevy Chevette (a term descended from **shittalay**), or any small car of inferior design. See also **toyolette.**

shittalay — Ford owner way to say the name of America's other most popular car.

shitting contest — when two motorists, who don't know each other from Adam, exchange unpleasantries with each other in an escalating spiral, often ending in violence. See also **FUJMO, middle finger salute, road rage.**

shootin' the drag — Nova Scotia way to say "driving up and down Main Street," a common amusement. In American Graffiti, it's **cruising.**

shoot the gap — cabbies in Guadalajara do this, to accompanying terror of their passengers. "To run the red light at big three-lane intersection"......dangerous as hell.

short — a car. California, underworld term.

massive **shorts** — such as, shorting the positive battery terminal to hood of car, or positive battery terminal to ground. Real fireworks here, since lots of "new" batteries have 500 amp/hr. ratings. We're talking sparks, *red hot* copper and metal (wrench, yer wrist watch, etc.) and battery giving off lots of hydrogen gas while this short happens. Remember the Hindenburg? And, if the battery blows up, add about 3/4 gallon of concentrated sulfuric acid blowing out of the battery case. You only have one face. Exercise care around batteries and high amperage electrical cables.

short sticking — when the gas station attendant (remember those?) checks yer oil, and carefully doesn't insert the dipstick all the way in, always coming up "a quart low, fraid so, buddy."

shot-gunning it — a practice all too common in the high-risk, exciting world of contemporary car repair. When the "mechanics" aren't really car repair diagnosticians but replace parts madly in the vicinity of the problem without finding out what the exact problem is and fixing it, they've "shotgunned it". Best way to deal with this practice is to carry one. See "how to keep from getting **cheated**".

shovel head — another Harley identified by the shape of the head. Looks sorta like an overturned shovel. See also **flat head, knuckle head, pan head, block head.**

show up on radar — to get airborne in car or motorcycle while going fast over a bump or rise.....in fact, to get very airborne (stadium motocross has some very steep jumps, which caused this observation to be made about Bob "Hurricane" Hannah).

shunt —"anytime cars touch during a race it is called a shunt but it is really a nice way of describing a wreck." —from C. H. B. in the San Antonio *Current* the day before the San Antonio Gran Prix (1988).

shut 'em down — to defeat in a drag race. "Little deuce coupe —-don't you know, you're going to shut them down" — Beach Boys song. "Deuce"—two door.

sidelights — parking lights (Brit).

sidestepping the clutch — while increasing the acceleration on a motorcycle, rotating the foot sideways on the clutch so it pops.

silencer — muffler (Brit.)

six-pack — three two-barrel carburetors, usually linked progressively. Also known as **three deuces.**

skid lid — a motorcycle helmet. Also called **skid pot.** See also **brain bucket, bone dome** (Brit.)

skids — old slang for "brakes" (from covered wagon days).

skid-wheels — casters installed on the back lower end of Winnebago type recreation vehicles (**RVs**), to keep it from dragging over uneven ground.

skids or turns over — there is in Austin, Texas a mall parking lot so big that you may give a car the ultimate handling test: you can drive it there so fast that it either "skids or turns over."

skipping — see **missing.**

Skoda — Czechoslovakian car appearing in England in quantity during the 1980s, the butt of many jokes. "What is a Skoda, really?" "A skip on wheels." (A "skip" is an urban garbage receptacle known in North America as a "dumpster.") "How do you double the value of your Skoda? Fill the tank with petrol." "Why do Skodas have rear window heaters? To keep your hands warm while pushing it." Skodas have fibre reverse gears which strip out.

slamming the door — a term from racing. Even being one tire's length ahead entitles one to cut across in front of another in a corner. This cornering maneouvre is also known as **closing the gate, shutting the door,** and **cutting him off.** Writing in the San Antonio *Current* the day before the 1988 San Antonio Gran Prix, C. H. B. says this maneuver is also familiar to San Antonio drivers off the racetrack. He also points out that it is a good way to start a post-race or post-rush hour fight.

slant six — well-known, fairly reliable Dodge-Plymouth-Chrysler six-cylinder engine, for such cars as the Valiant.

sleeper — a car that looks innocuous, looks stock or old and dilapidated, but is in fact heavily modified to produce power and performance. These cars may be spotted by the heavy uneven idling at stoplights.

sleeping policeman — irreverent term, in Belize, Mexico, and other Central American countries, for the **speed bumps** built into the pavement to slow drivers down in urban and residential areas. —from Lucio, the cabdriver of the "Texas Express," San Ignacio, Cayo District, Belize, C. A.

Our British informant reports that "in U. K. I believe they are those deadly spring-loaded spiked rails that can only be safely driven over in one direction—if you want to keep the pneu in your pneus." We are reserving judgment on whether this belief reflects reality or an urban legend (we grew up with nightmares that someone would actually invent and market such a device).

slicks — "treadless tires for maximum traction" —from C. H. B. in the San Antonio *Current* the day before the San Antonio Gran Prix (1988). Used in dry conditions. See **wets.**

slim-jim — flat strip of spring steel with notched, hooked ends to spring door mechanism open when slid into door along window glass. Essential equipment for police and urban car thieves.

"Slim jim" was also nickname for an unusually slender auto transmission in the 1962-64 Oldsmobiles.

To "jimmy" is an old term for "to pry open."

slingshot maneuver — using a leading car's draft to save power then whipping out from behind at the right moment and using the extra momentum to pass.

slipstreaming — a term for cars following each other closely to run a red light en masse at rush hour. Also used to describe running along a freeway close behind a big truck, to get the benefit of its wind-breaking effect. Also known as **tagging along.**

slitch — momentary interruption of electricity in solid state (transistor or i. c. component) stuff...i. e. your BMW on-board computer.

slow-death oil — too heavy a weight (10W-20W-30W etc) of oil in extreme winter. I. e., using 30W in conditions that call for 10W-20. Results in slow cranking, or no cranking, and slow death to your engine bearings due to "washout."

slung-a-rod — description of engine failure where rod bearing has failed and slipped out of place, causing a lot of noise. U.K.: "threw-a-rod."

slushbox — derogatory term for "automatic transmission." For the backboard off which this verbal shot was banked, see **o'matic.**

slut fuel filter — "Does your Toyota have the *slut fuel filter* or the *virgin fuel filter*," Greg asks. "I dunno", customer says, "what's the difference?"

"Well, the slut filter has her legs spread, like this...." Greg produces the little plastic fuel filter, its spigots pointing out at a wide (100 degree) angle. "Now the virgin filter," he says, producing another, "has her legs together....like this." "Well, I guess I have the slut." —Greg at International Car Parts, Austin TX, on the Toyota Corolla fuel filter.

slush box — automatic transmission.

smart transmission — automatic 4-speed tranny available in European cars such as BMW, Porsche, etc., which has a computer chip with connections to monitor speed, gas pedal action, cornering, etc. to shift the gears at exactly the right moment.

smish — diminutive of "smash," often used to describe a bent-in fender, grille, etc., which, when telling boyfriend, husband, mainsqueeze, homechop about it, minimizes the damage a little. Anything is better than saying "I smashed the fender." "I *smished* the fender" doesn't sound as bad.

smittys — actually, "Smithys," extinct, but legendary 50s glass pack mufflers, which, unlike today's stuff, got *better* with age. They started out sounding throaty at idle, with a snarl as you revved the motor... Then, after six months or so (after all the fibreglass had been blown out) they were *right*...that is, throbbing at idle, giving your old Ford V-8 that perfect nasty rasp cooking down country roads. You could jack the throttle in front of your girlfriend's house and cause her parents to say things like, "There is that damn Neil Hancock out front again in that loud Mercury."

smog pump — see **pollution control devices**

a **smoke** — London slang term for a "jalopy" or in Quebec, "un bazou." "What are you smoking these days?"

smoke show — holding the brakes on **and** spinning the tires.

smoke wrench — oxy-acetylene torch (it really helps to heat up a rusty or otherwise "frozen" nut).

Smokey — a policeman. Also known as "the **man", Smokey.** The origin of the CB term "bear" for policeman ("Smokey the Bear"—very old public cartoon character promoting fire safety practices).

smoke your tires — to **burn off, peel out.**

smoothing out the bumps — driving very fast down a rough dirt road, according to Uncle John Poteet—"you only hit the tops of the bumps."

smushed and compressed boll weevils — substance that Volvo timing gear (upper) is formed of. It is a fibre-formed gear, which runs silently but which about every three years strips the teeth off.

snake dance — Oklahoma slang for "making the drag," i. e. driving around the downtown square or area, and then wheeling back around and making it again.

snake in the grass — hidden radar trap. Also known as **lying in the weeds.**

snap-off tools — uncomplimentary term, especially among junkyard employees (who have to dismantle lots of rusty cars) for Snap-On Tools. See also **strap-on tools.**

sneakers — jocular term for unusually large tires, oversize tires. Also **boots.**

snick — Yuppie buzz word automotive writers are fond of using....in "Road Test" — "He snicked it into first gear and moved out." Gears do not "snick," they engage or crash.

snowbanker — a "Yank tank," a big American car, hard to control on snowy and icy roads, which ends up in the snowbanks and has to be towed out a lot. The term is used by Ken Dryden in *The Game*, to explain why sensible rules changes aren't made quickly in hockey and why hockey practices and customs change slowly. People who tend to follow the game with this slow-to-change attitude are "snowbankers."

snowbird — before Anne Murray's wonderful, famous song, this term meant "an abandoned car plowed into a snowbank." Also the chunk of ice that falls out from behind the wheel, as the **snowbird** drives south (a snowbird is also "a Quebecker in Florida in winter"). You may see the relationship, in time and meaning, of the two terms.

snowmobile — a term applied to the DeLorean, after John DeLorean, creator of the car, was caught in a cocaine sting.

soap dish — nickname for the early Porsche, from the shape of the body. See also **overturned soup spoon.**

Sob — Saab, as in "the customer told us another Sob story."

S. O. B. — very old, probably extinct competing product to STP oil treatment. Stands for "Stops Oil Burning." Thick, golden, viscous stuff, sold at gas stations in the 1960s.

soft parts — stuff that normally wears out, such as spark plugs, brake pads, water pumps, belts, etc. Usually available from auto parts stores. See **hard parts.**

S. O. L. — The auto airconditioning class instructor had been spitting loads of abbreviations at us all night, and this one would have gone right by except for one female who raised her hand. Admonishing us not to short out the E. C. M. ("electronic control module") by using a hot jumper wire on it, he used the abbreviation...."If you jump the E C M wif a hot wire you're S O L."

"What's S O L?" she squeaked. "Ahem, ma'am," he coughed, "you would be shit out of luck, because you would have **fried** the ECM...it would be burned up..... *history*."

sonic screamer — antitheft device, installed in car. When activated, by burglar, e. g., it goes off with a screech that is guaranteed by the manufacturers to make blood gush from offender's ears (and maybe even a few nearby ears at your apartment complex. Buy one and test it out on your neighbours, then get out of town.)

sound the oil — "check the oil" among fishermen in Cape Sable Island, Nova Scotia.

souped up — modified to produce maximum performance. A term especially used in the 1950s.

the **South Dallas device** — theoretical apparatus devised to protect the MGA sports car from hazards of parallel parking. A small, innocuous-looking thing mounted to front and rear bumpers. When small projecting finger is pushed by aggressor bumper, trip hammer is released, spring-loaded metal stamp strikes body work on aggressor car, stamping YOU HAVE JUST COME TOO CLOSE TO A SPORTS CAR, or HAVE A NICE DAY (or in Mexico City CHINGA TU PUTA MADRE, or VAYA A LA CHINGADA or simply TU MADRE.) {*Jim's note: The South Dallas device is not its name. This is another Steve Poteet theoretical device, to protect his MGA sports car. He named it the S. D. device after hisself,* **Stephen Dallas** *Poteet].*

go **south on you** — a way of saying that a car has suffered terminal engine failure. See also "**eat its lunch**." In some parts of Canada, especially the Eastern Townships of Quebec, the form is "go west on you."

spanner — British term for **wrench.**

spark plug fluid — phony item listed on a repair bill to pad it out. See also **muffler bearing, Johnson rod, Johnson box, Thelman bushing.**

speed shift — see **dab.**

spike — computer term come to Joe Mechanic. Big voltage surge when some component is switched off and resultant "spike" of voltage, stored in coil of relay, is let loose, to go through low voltage electronic control modules......

spinners — fake wire wheel hubcaps with knock-off headless nut with two little wings on it so a hammer could "spin" the wheel off. Highly prized and stolen a lot throughout the 1960s. Originally a race-car innovation, so that tires could be changed quickly.

spin out — to lose control of a car in a tight turn at high speed.

spoiler — 1) an **air-dam**

2) a sort of airplane wing on the back of **stock cars**, in imitation of racing car feature designed to keep the back down during high-speed races.

spontaneous combustion — everyone, or almost everyone, knows that the key to the unholy marriage of fire, iron, electricity, and liquids known as a car is the "internal combustion" engine. The trick is to keep the combustion internal: all good mechanics think a lot more about the possibility of "spontaneous combustion", because oily rags left in the sun on car seats with the windows rolled up can and may catch fire without any spark. And you better believe it, buddy.

spookin' — riding around in a car without any particular purpose or destination. 1950s, U. S.

spooling up — "the process of a turbo winding up to its maximum rpm and therefore maximum output." —from CHB. As the interface is air-driven, not mechanically, there is a slight lag. From airplane turbo engine talk.

sport mode — one of two settings, i. e. this one is "on," of the steering and suspension damper in the Mazda RX-7 car made necessary by the twisting torque effect of the rotary engine when the driver puts the **pedal to the metal.** See also **Porsche baiter** and **economy mode.**

sports car — John Lawlor's superb *How to talk car, the* guide to hot rods and drag racing (1965), admits the difficulty of defining this term, but offers "an automobile engineered for driving satisfaction rather than passenger comfort," and points out that the "two-seater body" is usual. He gives as examples the MG-B and Triumph TR-4, the Corvette and the Mustang, but claims the Oldsmobile Starfire is not one.

Our anonymous British car fan informant defines a sports car as "seats no more than two, and has no roof." He offers the Miata as example.
See also **roadster** and **open tourer.**

Spridget — Austin-Healey, owned by British Motor Corporation, which in 1955 bought MG, made the MG Midget, which, along with all Sprites except the first (the **Bugeye**), were dubbed "Spridget."

spritzer — slang term for a fuel injector, the device replacing the carburetor more and more in high-performance engines.

spun — bearing. Condition, fatal, where a bearing seizes up completely and irresistible force meets and spins immovable object — ripping and tearing the bearing mount, crankshaft, etc.

spun-a-main — main bearing failure, usually caused by lack of oil or oil pressure. Terminal problem for the motor.

squeegies — treaded rain tires, for racing.

squirrelly — like the name implies, tends to jump around, from excess wheel spin. Hard to control within the power band. See **peaky.**

stab and steer driver — in racing, an unsmooth driver. He stabs his way into corners or situations and attempts to steer his way out of them.

stale green — said of a green light seen from far enough ahead to know that it is likely to turn yellow before you get there. Particularly and probably originally a truckers' term, especially truckers who drove the big rigs transporting natural gas, as for them a "stale green" was a definite danger, a sign to start braking right away! —from Dewey Poteet, formerly with Texas Gas Transport, later known as Pressure Transport, and now in less dangerous work in San Antonio.

'stang — Mustang. See also **cop 'stang.**

starting juice — ether in a spray can, which because it ignites rapidly, may be sprayed in the carburetor to aid in starting a car which will **crank over** but won't fire.

station wagon — these inevitable American cars, which handle, brother Dewey says, as if a telephone pole were sticking 25 feet out the rear, were named, according to Cecil Adams' "Straight Dope" column, in the horse and carriage business. First known as "depot wagons," before 1890, they were "four-wheeled covered vehicles that you might take down to the railroad station to pick up passengers and their baggage....some with removable back seat and a tailgate that could be lowered to facilitate loading, ...also wood sides...and ungainly designs, [making them] look like orange crates on wheels."]

"steamboat-bridge" rear windows — a key feature of the **"greenhouse" four-door hardtop convertible** of the years 1959-60, according to the Cool Car Club News (Austin TX, Sept.-Oct. 1988). See also **Vista, Holiday.**

steering with the throttle — maneuver whereby you enter a curve fast, cock the thing over into a slide, and apply gas, breaking the rear wheels loose and letting the slide point you in the direction you should go (i. e. rear end comes around pointing you, rather than actually steering in the direction you should go). Fun, in the snow, when you're alone on a wide road, or in an empty parking lot.

Ex-dirt racer Jim Poteet (on curves): "Sit up on the gas tank, grab a big handful of throttle.....hang the ass end out, and steer with the throttle."

I'd rather **step in shit than work on that car** — said by a mechanic refusing to work on a car, like, say, a Lincoln. The implication is that working on these cars would be the equivalent or worse.....

stick you to the seats — what a really good (or foolish) driver can do to you in a fast, high-performance car.

sticky toilet paper — see **S. T. P.**

Sting Ray — Corvette. Ever see one of these involved in a collision? Fiberglass body spreads impact over entire body, shattering it into lots of pieces....lots of picking up by wrecker driver.

stink bomb — a used car that just won't sell because of an offensive odor (dog piss, humans living in the back seat too long, etc.)

stock — as originally designed, manufactured, and sold by the car maker. Anything else is **custom.**

S. T. O. P. — acronym for "squeal tires on pavement".
In the province of Quebec, STOP signs have been caught up in a graffitti-borne public debate over the political issue of the language of signs. Ignoring the fact that "Stop" is now both an English and a French (from France) word, Quebec linguistic purists prefer "Arret." So when the Supreme Court of Canada declared the province's French-only sign law (Bill 101) unconstitutional, some separatist

activists artfully modified a lot of Montréal STOP signs, painting out the "S", the top of the "T", and the loop on the "P" to make them read "101". However, by a sort of Murphy's Law of graffitti, an imperfectly executed modification may convey the reverse meaning of that intended: this one signals STOP 101, in the harsh semiotics of the experienced eye. Or, as Martin Stone of the Montréal *Gazette* suggests, it sends the subliminal message "ARRET 101", surely an expression of the ambivalence of Québec to equal the almost evenly divided vote for "Oui" and "Non" in the referendum on separation.

stoppie — formed on the analogy of **wheelie,** in bike talk, a controlled, maintained lifting of the rear wheel under braking. Or, an unintentional effect of extreme front braking, which lifts the rear wheel off, possibly so much as to cause an **endo.** ***Do not go out and try this yourself. (Editor)***

stovebolt six — Chevrolet engine, also known as the **hotwater six.**

S. T. P. — "The Racer's Edge." "You know that thick yellow stuff seals rings, restores lost engine pep, etc. Did you know that if you pour some in a jar and you catch a fly and put it in the STP and watch it go down into it...did you know that fly will be in there forever?"

"Yes," I answer, "but did you know that when you poured it into your BMW, it stopped the oil pump so hard it snapped the oil pump drive chain?"

"Is that why it stopped the way it did?" she asks.

"That's right."

Also known as "Sticky Toilet Paper." See also **S. O. B.**

strap-on tools — other (affectionate) name of most famous and best of all mechanics' hand tools (Snap-On). But see also **snap-off tools.**

street legal — equipped with all necessary features to pass inspection, i. e. lights, horn, emergency brake, etc. Many of these items are unnecessary weight on a drag- or any other racer, but the police seem to think they are important for cars that drive around town or out on the highway.

street rod — a **chopped and channeled**, **souped up hot rod,** especially in the '50s. "A 1948 and older modified car." —from Paul Burrill, Madison WI.

street squirrel — a kid who races around on his moped as if it were a Harley or other big motorcycle.

stretch — a "stretch" was the common term in New York in the late 1980s for a stretch limousine, according to Blaze Starr, who was doing publicity touring to promote the film about her relationship with Governor Earl Long of Louisiana.

strip — to dismantle a stolen car, taking off parts with any value. See **chop shop.**

strip the gears — to knock teeth off the gear wheel by inefficient shifting while the motor is revving. Usually only a tooth or two is knocked off, so "strip" is a metaphor, possibly sexual.

stroked — said of an engine which has increased displacement due to lengthened stroke. Done by welding up crankshaft lobes, then grinding them round again, making the crankshaft throw longer, thus lengthening the stroke. See also **bored.** Often used together, "bored and stroked," to increase engine "size", i. e. power, internally.

Stromberger — A Stromberg carburetor.

strummed — engine tuned and boosted to the utmost (as in Formula I racing, where 1500ccs will develop around 1200 hp, from a turbo with intercooler, tuned intake and exhaust, etc. Also said of lots of race car engines whose owners would rather go real fast rather than have a reliable engine.

Studillac, Studelack — A Studebaker Skyliner with a Cadillac V-8 engine. The only problem was keeping a transmission between this powerful motor and the wheels....Perhaps the ultimate muscle car.....the only cheap way you could win drag races.....cost maybe $300 in parts, if you did the work yourself.....a used engine, a pickup truck rear axle.....

stupid-baker — Studebaker. Actually these little cars, which looked the same from the front and the back, were quite reliable; the Studebaker Lark was the first compact car; the Golden Hawk had a supercharged engine; the 1953 Skyliner coupe was the first car in the Museum of Modern Art, for its design. Its disappearance, after it was bought out by Packard, was a loss. The Big Three American car manufacturing firms, Ford, GM, Chrysler, were popularly supposed to have driven out the competition.

Known as "Portuguese cars" in Brazil, (from their appearing to go both ways), where the folk from the old country are their Newfies.

suck the headlights out of it — said of a spectacular high-speed pass. See also **blow his doors off.**

S. U. fuel pump — on most British cars. Notoriously balky and unreliable. Best remedy is to hit it repeatedly with "the open palm" as the book says, until it clicks back on. "A decent length of wood needed to be carried in a Mini as the pump was at the front of the bottom of the tank. The necessary blow, up and under, between the rear wheels, would have painful, obscene overtones that caused most male viewers to wince!" —our anon. Brit.

submarine flush toilet — incredibly enough, the adjustment instructions for the BMW 2002 Tii fuel injection pump linkages correspond exactly to captured German U-boat manuals "how to" on the john. (Mechanics' nickname for the old Kugel-Fisher mechanical fuel injection pump which fuels the godawful fast BMW 2002 Tii.)

suction type wipers — until the middle 1950s, cars had engine vacuum-operated windshield wipers, rather than the electric-motor type almost universal on automobiles now.

Suck-u-matic — see **Vacuumatic.**

suicide bars — antisway bars, a custom option on high performance cars that gives much more stability, up to a point; at that point, the irresistible force overpowers the immovable object, and the car skids or turns over.

suicide clutch — from vintage motorcycle days, old Indian Chiefs and Harleys came fitted with "rocker" foot clutch pedals (in and out). By rocking heel you disengaged clutch until the toe rocked it in. The "suicide" modification was simply to eliminate rocker, replacing it with a simple foot pedal, spring-loaded; so, sitting at stoplight, with right foot on pavement, balancing very heavy machine, left foot depressing clutch pedal, handshift lever in first gear, if someone should bump yer motorcycle from rear, or if balance was tipped, causing your left foot to come off pedal.....machine would lunge forward into cross traffic. Hence the term "suicide" clutch. —from Andy Anderson, famed pinstripe artist and antique motorcyclist.

suicide door — rear door that opened to the front, e. g. the old Lincoln limousine, various Fiats. Opened at speed, would no doubt be ripped away at the hinges. "Any door hinged at the rear, opens at the front, i. e. '33 and '34 Fords" : —from Paul Burrill, Madison WI.

suicide seat — the right-hand front seat of a vehicle. To occupy this seat is often called **riding shotgun.**

suicide pegs — on an easy-rider sort of motorcycle, with side bars in front of the seat, pegs so the driver may rest his feet up ahead and look cool. Only thing is, he can't brake or downshift quickly in that position.....

sump — British term for "oil pan."

needs a **sunroof on the floorboard** — said of the Suzuki Samurai, because they turn over so easily.

supercharging — came from airplanes first, where the thin air of altitude flying made it useful, and increased performance besides. See also **turbo supercharging.**

surf car — a true surf car (as opposed to those shiny new Samurais driven by brain-damaged smiling fools on TV), according to Minor Wilson, residing near the beach on Maui, is something like a 65 Chevy with big rust holes coming through lots of places in the body, and instead of fancy surfboard racks, has 2 by 4s bolted directly to the roof with big nuts and bolts.

Like a faithful old dog, the surf car sits patiently on the beach, letting the salt and sand eat it, while patiently waiting for the surfers to finish up....the last blast, the wind just before sunset, and head back into town.

Famous surf cars: "Blue Heaven."

He was poking the 12-volt test light around under the dashboard. "Hell, all you have to find is a live wire," he muttered. Curtis, Greg's roommate, was hooking up an old 8-track stereo in "Blue Heaven," a 1964 Ford Fairlane, the third sound system, after AM-FM radio and cassette tape deck. With both doors open, shirt off, beer in hand, Curtis was confident of success.

"All right," he whoops, "I've found one." And, after he spliced in the 8-track's wires, the deck blared. "Damn," he muttered, "this cassette won't eject. I guess we'll have only 'Best Hits of Beach Boys' on this deck..." This was cool with Greg, and the two jumped into "Blue Heaven" to come over to my place, only to discover that the Beach Boys were extinguished by the closing of the doors.

"I guess the live wire you found was the one to the dome light," Greg observes. "Yeah," Curtis mutters. "I guess we can use it when we're parked...at parties....or at the lake....just open the doors....We sure as hell can't lissen to it while driving."

I heard "Blue Heaven" chug up the driveway and shut off. And then, blaring forth as the grinning duo emerged from the car....."Well, she got her Daddy's car and she headed for the hamburger stand now......da dat da da dada da ta da....." and then abrupt silence as the doors shut.

"Did you rig it up that way on purpose?" I asked.

"Hell, no," he says. "But it's great, isn't it?" Opens door — "and she forgot all about the library like she told her old man now......" Closes door (silence).

Everyone loved it...left at near top volume, the arrival of Blue Heaven and its wild occupants was thenceforth announced by the Beach Boys best hits.

surging — common modern complaint of out of tune cars. "It feels as if someone else was giving it the gas and backing it off." Caused by improper fuel/air ratio, clogged air filter, bad oxygen sensor, fuel injectors that can't find the right level, etc.

sushimobile — Japanese car. Also **fishheads, riceburners.**

suspenders — struts, suspension units. "It's time to replace the old suspenders!"

swallow a valve — after a valve is very worn down, so that it is smaller, parts of it can actually be sucked into the cylinder, causing the motor to **eat its lunch.** See also **float the valves.** --from Martin Stone.

Old VWs do this quite a lot. Swallowing a valve usually happens when air intake leaks (air cooled VWs have no head gasket) lean out the mixture; resultant blow-torch-like effect weakens the valve stems....and when the valve stem breaks, valve face drops into the works (piston, other valve) and engine "scatters" with resultant shrapnel, black oil smoke, etc. Also known as "drop a valve." See **grenading.**

swap holes — what Harley pistons do when over-**revved**.

swapping paint jobs — used by an ESPN commentator while viewing a Long Beach, CAlif. road race where comedian Jay Leno repeatedly sideswiped Toyota teammate's car.

Can happen on a track too: "driving in his first major race in 1975, The Atlanta 500, Ricky Rudd crashed into the wall. Certain his car was about to blow up, Ricky scrambled out and jumped over the pit wall. Then an official strolled up and told him, 'All you did was scrape a little paint off your car. Now get out there and move it, because it's blocking the track!" — Nash & Zullo, *Sports Hall of Shame* (syndicated cartoon), February 11, 1990.

sweetening — Genteel British word for what is known in South Texas as **finishing school.**

T

taco wagon — a car decorated with all sorts of cheap cosmetic modifications that don't affect its handling but are considered fashionable among Mexican American automobilists. The **low rider** feature was peculiar to the taco wagon. Also pinstripes in paint job, fur on dashboard, plastic Jesus for dashboard, fringe with little balls hanging down from front window top margin, little colored lights for back window, furry dice to dangle from rear view mirror. See also **tamale boat.**

tagging along — see **slipstreaming.**

tags — license plates.

tailgate party — at an outdoor sporting event, a party held on the tailgate of a pickup, with beer, pimento cheese sandwiches, etc. taken out of icechests which are sitting on the tailgate.

tailgating — following another car much too close. Also known as **bird-dogging.** Note: if you insist on doing this, close up real tight. If A brakes, you'll hit him at about 1/2 mph relative speed before you let his brakes do the slowing for both of you. Stay glued.

tail-happy — describes the behaviour of a powerful car without much weight in the back seat. See **steering with the throttle.**

taillight guarantee — the guarantee is good until you can't see the taillights no more. Like the **out of sight guarantee, around the block guarantee.**

Taiwan taxis — in Taiwan, cyclists like to ride as close as possible to the taxicabs, for, as they say, "good luck", with the further explanation that if you're really close but not being run over, they won't run over you; another explanation is that if they run over your shadow, you know they're not running over you. Another new tradition of the new age: wake up, America, smell the coffee; how automobiles and less polluting forms of transportation may coexist on Mother Earth.

talking K car — Chrysler's K car talks. A micro-chip-controlled robot-like voice warns you "Your

door is ajar," "Please fasten your seat belt," etc. Voted most likely to be the first damn thing to be unplugged by car owners.
"Homer," he says, "this new K-car I just bought yesterday....can I bring it by and have yer man disconnect its voice...that damn voice is bothering Ethel something fierce......"
Note to K-car owners: try this for a bit of fun and robot-torture. Leave doors ajar, belts unfastened, hood and trunk open, etc.....Then start the car. Robot chip will advise you.....squawking faster and faster, going through its entire repertory of stuff......

tall gearbox — said of cars like Toyota, which are geared for high speed with good power. Specifically, overdrive, 5th gear give a car a **tall** gearbox.

tamale boat — nickname for a car fixed up by Mexican-Americans the way they like it: say, a 1978 Chevy station wagon mainly rust and primer gray colored, at least one door tied on with clotheshanger or multicolored rope, at least one cracked window. See also **taco wagon.**

tank slapper — a motorcyclist's worst nightmare — a speed wobble in which the handlebars oscillate back and forth wildly...sometimes you come out of this sort of thing....sometimes you lose control and crash. And when a motorcycle loses control at speed, it sometimes causes the rider to slap the tank, inevitably with a sensitive part of the anatomy. "His crash today was a real tank slapper." It can literally dent the tank, both sides.

tankers — a name for certain **lakesters**, early drag racing machines in which the body was made out of reused aircraft belly fuel tanks. Also known as **belly tankers.**

tappet — English term for the part between the pushrod (the "lifter", the "rocker") and rocker arm, which serves by actually "tapping" the valves open. Can be hydraulic. "I've never understood why the 'rocker boxes' are where they are this side of the pond. One 'opened up the "rocker box" to 'adjust the tappets."' —our anon. Brit.

Named for Ted Tappet, a name used in the 1950s by racing driver Phil Hill.

"When I nod my head, you tap it with the hammer!"

target — or "police target." A **bad boy car,** a car without a hood, loud muffler, etc.

tattle tale — "special tachometer which records the highest engine speed reached during an individual run or lap...to find out how hard an engine is being pushed." — John Lawlor, *How to talk car*. The driver is free to watch the course, but the reading allows, among other things, finding out after the race which driver over-**revved** the team car!

tatty — British term for an old motorcycle, from the British word for "slightly worn." "Tatty Talk" is a column in a British motorcycle magazine dealing with such matters as how to stop leaks, etc.

Tazio — to "do a Tazio" is to do a successful **balls to the wall** manoeuvre, like passing on the inside on wet pavement. Named after Tazio Nuvolari, famous Italian racing driver.

T-boning — spectacular accident in which one car rams another from the side, in the middle. A term from races on figure-8 racetracks, where such accidents are not only possible, but expected by the crowd. Also known as **center punching.**

tech inspection — "scrutineering" (U.K.) Sports car owners who are considering racing their cars would be well advised to obtain a copy of the SCCA (Sports Car Club of America) "General Competition Rules," read it, and go over the car before being tech inspected and rejected. Certain safety modifications must be made. For example, cars equipped with carburetors with "swaged" fuel inlet fittings (where the fuel pipe is just hammered into a hole in the carb body....and can come out in heat of competition) must have same pipe removed, have threads tapped into the carb body, and fuel inlet pipe securely screwed in. These guys don't want you to get hurt, or to hurt anyone. It is alleged that sports car races are safer than driving on the street. You are, after all, racing others with your engine size (or very close to it), everyone has crash helmets, etc. Anyone who has been on the Houston Freeway at rush hour knows what we're talking about. It's everyone for his/er self on Friday afternoon.

teething troubles — problems experienced by a novice racing driver (a **yellow bumper**).

tender — rusty, weakened by corrosion. Nova Scotia term.

ten tenths — driving the (race) car at its absolute limits, which can be quickly followed by "eleven tenths". See **shunt**.

test drive — 1960s slang for car theft....often the event turned out to be a real test drive, too: youth bragged of record times (15 minimum) they drove the car as FAST as it would go.....then stop as hard as it could be stopped....then a furious series of putting it into reverse, then "drive", then reverse, then "drive," and so on. The poor car squeals tires and jerks back and forth like a huge drunk robot. Kids in the 60s stole automatic transmission cars for kicks (if you stole someone's **muscle car,** you might get 1) caught, 2) hurt, 3) caught and *hurt.* See **joy ride.**

test spot, test track, test strip — usually a flat, clear freeway over a long bridge, where you may open 'er up without danger of getting a ticket. The bridge is good because a cop coming from the opposite direction can't turn around, and a flat, clear freeway has no niche for a radar trap. The situation can change at any moment, if an **eye in the sky** helicopter is around, or a disguised radar cop car, but the physical requirements are at least half to three-quarters of a mile visibility, no exit or on ramps, flat and straight road with no billboards. Once police become aware that a **test spot** exists, it's over (tickets by camera using new Ka band radar).

Tetrasone-Atmosite — gasket cement. Artie and I puzzled over this one for almost an hour. The Zundapp overhaul manual clearly calls for a layer of tetrasone-atmosite between the engine cases upon assembly. Mythical, probably extinct, absolutely unavailable *foreign* gasket cement. Solution: use the local stuff, **elephant snot.** See also **gorilla snot.**

Texas start — in SCCA racing, a rolling start is called informally a "Texas start" when the whole group of cars stampedes, jumping the gun all together.

the Car — Los Angeles Police Department's armored car, used as a battering ram to break down house doors, walls, etc., in surprise raids.

Thelman bushing — phony part named to pad the bill for an unsuspecting and naive customer.

thingamajigger — name given to any part or object you can't remember the right name for. Also **clyde, doomaflockie, chingadera, chingaso.**

the patience of a **thousand monks** — "you must acquire it," older mechanic to his apprentice. "Do I have the patience of 100 monks yet?" he asks. "You have the patience of 100 gerbils," he growls. "Get back to work!"

thrash — the racing equivalent to an 'all-nighter,' i. e. bringing a problem or damaged car up to specifications.

three deuces — three two-barrel carburetors, usually linked progressively. Also **a six-pack.** See **father-son switch.**

three-legged dog — an eighteen-wheeler with one set of wheels lifted off the pavement, because it's running empty or with a light load and doesn't need the full support of all the running gear.

three on a tree — stickshift. (Nova Scotia)

three-wheelers — In the 1980s, this term identifies a kind of motorcycle. But much earlier, there was a car, the Morgan V-twin, motorcycle engined, three-wheeled, the two in front steerable, the motor mounted on the outside, in front of the bonnet, dating from the 1920s. The **Isetta** is another example.

three-window coupe — "a two-door, two passenger car—only the door windows and the rear window are counted." —from Paul Burrill, Madison WI. See also **five window coupe.**

threshold of pain — more than 150 decibels, according to Lakewaves Stereo, causes permanent ear damage (when the windows are pulsating in and out).

thromp — as in "thromped the accelerator", a combination of "tromp" and "throttle"? Found in Alan Foster's *Alien Nation*, pg. 183.

throttle body fuel injection — already eclipsed by port fuel injection. Little better than a carburetor.

thumper — a single cylinder four-stroke motor. —from Chris Coyle. A large engine with four or fewer cylinders, e. g. Norton 500 cc single cylinder bikes, 4 cylinder Pinto engines, etc. So called because these engines are not inherently balanced and so they get rough when pushed hard. **One-lunger.**

Thunderlizard — see **AC.**

Thunder Road — timeless Robert Mitchum film. Crime doesn't pay-bootleg runner-car film. Aptly demonstrates lack of handling ability of Ford sedans of the 1950s. Get beer and see this one at the drive-in.

ticket mill — a town so named because of frequent speed traps. (The dingummed city of Austin is such a burg).

Tiger — the Sunbeam Tiger, now extinct but a remarkable car in its day. It was a British-made car with a Ford 260 V-8 engine that would "light up the tires for a block." Also wore rear wheel bearings out and had bad understeer.

tiger — GM advertising department's original nickname for Pontiac GTO (which, as we all know, became the "**judge**" or "**goat**"). Source for all the above entries—General Motors—First 75 Years", by editors of *Automobile Quarterly.*

tightened — "It's been tightened," in California, means "it's been made a bunch faster," by increased turbo boost, upped compression, or the like.

time bomb — sounds like one, may turn into one: an electric fuel pump from Canadian Tire bought and installed by a teenager in the trunk near the gas tank. It ticks and gurgles.

tin lizzie — a Model T Ford.

tits — top-notch, in very good shape. "This car is just tits!" "How's it running? Tits, man."

toilet — car dealers' word for any very dirty used car. (It is interesting to note that in Moscow, a dirty car can get a ticket for that offense.)

ton — 100 mph, hence, to "do the ton." (U. K.)

tonneau cover, tonneau — snap-on cover for 'cockpit' of sports car, usually with fore and aft zip to leave passenger side covered when driving solo.

un **tonne de beurre** — Quebec French slang expression for "Thunderbird." Literally means "a ton of butter."

ton-up kid — early U. K. rocker, with more oil on his hair than in the sump. A would-be Elvis—on a Triumph Tiger, nose down, arse up.

tool man — Snap-On, Mac, etc., sell tools, give away girlie calendars.

to **tool someone** — a measure of how pervasive car talk is in North America, this term has been adapted to mean "to kid, to lie in order to have fun." A **tool job.** I. e. "When I was a kid I got my finger up my nose all the way to the second knuckle, and had to go to the doctor to get it extracted." "I don't believe it," she says, "you're a tool job." "Well," he says, "did you know that once every one million times when humans mate they get stuck together, like dogs, and can't get apart until they get water squirted on them?" "It happened to me with my last boyfriend," she says, smiling. "I got so pissed off I dragged him outside into the yard, him screaming and upside down..... the neighbours all came out." "You tool job," he says.

topless — used car salesman's term for convertible. "Come see this one, Leroy," he was saying into the phone, "it's a 1979 Chevy...topless!"

Topolino — Italian for "little mouse," this **beercan car** was a 600cc air-cooled twin built by Fiat. Before 1940, 500cc. Surprising amount of roominess.

torque — an ordinary technical term in mechanics which has been adapted for general use to describe someone who is "all wound up," very angry or tense: "he's all torqued up over that business."

to **total** a car — to wreck it completely, so that it is a "total loss." The term comes from insurance, but is used to describe any terminal wreck.

totaled — very common term for "wrecked." This term originally comes from the world of car insurance, a "total loss." Of course the car may be repaired, but the insurance company considers that the cost would be more than the car is worth.

Toyolette — perhaps inevitable nickname for the Chevrolet Nova, built by Toyota and Chevrolet joint corporation (Numi) in California. Also applied to the Toyota Land Cruiser, body by Toyota and Chevy V-8 power plant.

toy otter — parts men's term for Toyota.

Trabi — East German car, according to Miriam Widman, "a tiny, inefficient, and polluting automobile." But butt of many jokes: How do you double the value of a Trabi? Fill it with gas. How many people do you need to build a Trabi? Three: one cuts, one folds, and one glues. How do you tell the difference between the sport model of the Trabi and the regular one? The sport model has a pair of sneakers in the trunk. A Trabi and a donkey meet at a crossway. The Trabi says, "Guten Tag. I'm a car." The donkey says, "Guten Tag. I'm a horse."

A Rolls hits a Mercedes, then a Trabi hits the Rolls. The Mercedes driver says "This accident will cost me a month's income." The Rolls driver says, "For me it will be ten months' income." The Trabi driver says, "For me it will be at least 10 years' income." The two others ask, "Why did you buy such an expensive car?"

traction bars — bars which run from the front frame to the rear axle on drag racers, to keep the leaf springs from being torn out when the car squats as it takes off. The effect is to lock the suspension. Also known as **ladder bars.** Designed to prevent or at least resist **wheel-hop.**

tradeoff — when you put a hot cam in a car you get a tradeoff: your engine doesn't pull as hard at low rpm (it "lopes" etc.), but it goes like blazes at higher rpm. Less power at low rpm means higher power at high rpm.

trail throttle oversteer — a vehicle which, in turns during racing, will spin out, rear end thrown out trying to pass the front, "if you don't keep the throttle on!"

tranny — transmission.

tranny cannon — mythical tool for installing a tranny.

tran-o-mite — to rhyme with "dynamite," a mythical tool for removing a tranny.

transient — momentary bad reading of an electrical gauge due to fluctuation in load or momentary short. Technicians at infamous Three Mile Island nuclear power plant said that they didn't activate emergency procedures right at once because they thought it was a "transient" reading. This error caused the meltdown that cost millions of dollars.

TravTek — for "Travel Technology," one of several "smart car" systems for navigation and control assistance to help move traffic in congested areas. "A $12-million, one-year test that is about to wind up in Orlando FLA, it is considered the most comprehensive of the lot, because of the route-planning, navigation and other services it gives drivers." —Timothy Pritchard, "Smart Cars down the road," Toronto *Globe and Mail* (February 1, 1993). See also **Pathfinder, Prometheus, Drive.**

tree-frog — insulting nickname describing the 1990 Porsche, because media and customers did not like its new design. The result was the appearance of **kit car** versions like the Spexter, designed by Paul Deutschman of Westmount, Québec and built by Reeve Callaway of Old Lyme, Conn.

those little **triangular orange signs** — required by law to be displayed on the back of farm vehicles on the highway. According to a report on Morning Edition, National Public Radio, October 27, 1988, some Amish people in Pennsylvania are challenging the law on the grounds that the signs are "worldly objects" which violate their religious beliefs.

tricked out — old, possibly overused slang from 70s, to mean a car which is souped up or has performance-enhancing suspension modifications, or is all fucked up from such modifications.

Triumph — the car: now that they're gone, we can talk about them.

"Adjust clutch," the repair order said. Peter and I had looked it over, jacked it up. I called him back. "Sir," I said, "you better come down here and take a look....The transmission casing has broken in half, just behind the clutch." Oil leaking, gear crunching, Lucas electricity, is it any wonder they became extinct?

troops — a lot of mechanics were in the military. In many shops the boss can still yell out "all right, line up, troops," and they will. "Let's see you guys get this place real clean before you go home!"

TR-Sex — Triumph TR-6. Similarly, Triumph GT-Sex.

tubbo, turdo — slang names for turbo-charged car.

Tucker — innovative car of the 1940s, only 51 of them made. Powered by helicopter engine, air-cooled, rear engined luxury car which could do 100mph in the days when most could manage 45-50mph. "Highest power-to-weight ratio yet seen on a U.S. car, independent 4-wheel suspension, disk brakes." The center headlight swivelled with the front wheels. Driven out by the American Big Three, who controlled steel supply, and Senator Homer "Milktoast" Ferguson of Michigan, who started a Securities and Exchange fraud investigation of the company. —from Cool Car Club newsletter, Austin TX, Sept.-Oct. 1988. Now a major movie.

tudor — a two door, four passenger, car.

tuk-tuk — Thai/Hong Kong mode of transport/taxi. One cylinder, putt-around motorized rickshaw (name is onomatopoeic—sounds like what it is).

tumba burros — A Mexican term for the old familiar "cow-catcher", i. e. a bar or set of bars on the front of a heavy vehicle to bounce animals out of the way. Means "knocks down burros." An Australian variety is the **roo bar.**
Seen on the front of a New Mexico truck, labelled as such.

tuned up — this common term for the careful adjustment of all variables so that a car runs perfectly and smoothly suggests the association of harmonious mechanics and music: see **coming on the pipe, coming on song.** It also finds its way into Nova Scotia talk, as "half tuned up" there means "quite drunk."

tunes — in the phrase "that car is worth the price: it has tunes," the word refers to a good radio or tape deck.

tunnel ram — see **high rise intake.**

turbo supercharging — has taken over the technology because there is no mechanical connection between the motor and the mechanism which compresses the gas/air mixture. Exhaust gases are cycled through an impeller which does the packing: thus it's an air interface, unlike the early superchargers, which used a set of cams, gears, and valves, cumbersome and unreliable, and productive of enormous additional noise. See **Blower Bentley.**

turd-bird — derogatory nickname for the Ford Thunderbird.

turn-key car — in advertising of used cars (or sometimes even new car) a term for a car that is ready to drive away. "Only $4950 for this turn-key car!"

to **turn shit into gold** — a long restoration of a really dilapidated classic sports car, culminating in

a beautiful smooth running car and the resultant payoff large, the time taken often enormous.
Also used to describe an almost impossible job, repair of an **orphan** sports car, i. e. one which is no longer made.
turret-top — all-steel convertible top, removable, no cloth insert.

the **turtle** — old slang for "the trunk" or "the trunk lid.

turtle up — just as in nautical language, to overturn and end up wheels skyward.

twice pipes and quad device — twin exhaust and four 2-barrel carburetors.

twingle — nickname for the old Puch motorcycle, powered by a "twin single," a two-piston, 2-stroke engine with a common combustion chamber.

twist its tail — to make a car perform, driving it very fast.

two-percenter — tag embroidered onto jackets, tattooed on the skin, or otherwise proudly applied and worn by outlaw bikers in response to the statement, in the early 70s, by the president of the American Motorcycle Association to the effect that "98% of all American motorcyclists are decent, hardworking, law-abiding citizens." See also **one-percenters.**

two-step — when two race cars lock bumpers and spin around and around, as in dancing.

U-Z

ugly duckling — a Renault, also known as **deux chevaux** ("two horses").

unaware sensor — what parts men call a wear sensor (for braking system) to tell the unaware (but wary) driver that it is time to replace his brake pads.

understeer — the opposite of "oversteer" (see **trail throttle oversteer**), this tendency in handling may be described as "plowing," the front end failing to respond well to the steering intention. This feature is the reason why Corvettes don't make good race cars. V-8 engines, from sheer imbalance of weight in the front end, tend to create understeering. Before the independent rear wheel suspension Sting Ray model, Corvettes had a severe problem with oversteering, too: stiff suspension and too much power made the rear wheels **break loose** easily.

unglued — "damaged or destroyed, esp. an engine or transmission which has blown." — from John Lawlor, *How to talk car.*
Also, to lose traction, spin out, slide off, etc. "Come unglued."

unintended acceleration — lawsuits flew over this phenomenon, by terrified and some bandaged owners of Audi 5000 automatics. But see **driveway rocket.**

unmarked car — a police car which looks like a ordinary car. A **ghost car.**

unobtainium — mysterious, wonderful material much sought after, rumored to fix anything, seal all gaskets, etc. Turns out not to have been made since 1937, and then only in Rio.

unsafe at any speed — this term, the title of a book by Ralph Nader which suggests the general possibility of faulty cars on the road, was actually coined to describe a specific car, the 1968 Corvair, for reasons which should be obvious to anyone who has ever driven one.

upside down — new car salesman's phrase for a fact about the new world of new car prices: "Before the 41- to 45-month term on that 60-month loan, you owe more than the car is worth. That's called being 'upside down.' After 41 to 45 months, you owe less than the car is worth....We see people every-day who are $2500 to $3500 upside down on their car......The 60-month loan was brought out four to five years ago [in 1990] as car prices went higher. The higher the cost, the more the payments had to be stretched out so that people could afford a car."—Craig Bernard, owner of a string of dealerships in Illinois, quoted in Jim Mateja, Chicago Tribune (Jan. 1990). See also **New car salesman, green pea, note lot.**

upside down bathtub — frequent description of the 1949-51 Nash. "Jellybean" was another.

urban surfin' — swerving out of your lane and up onto the sidewalk or someone's yard. Also known as **curb surfin'.**

U-turn — the longest U-turn in history: In a Rolls-Royce Corniche, Stanley Sedgwick in 1973 drove from Dunkirk to Marseilles and back between morning coffee and dinner. —from Fox and Smith, *Rolls-Royce: The Complete Works.*

UV damage — also "sun fade." Rubber shrinkage, plastic turning brittle and cracking, all from ultraviolet rays of the sun.

V

Vacuumatic — one of the many names affixed to automatic transmissions. This one got dubbed **suck-u-matic.**

valve job — "refacing the valves to get better sealing." —Robert Appel, *The Used Car Believer's Handbook.*

vapor lock — usually happens to hot engine. Interruption of fuel flow to carburetor caused by bubbles in fuel lines or pump. The old South Austin cure for vapor lock: "Pour a cold beer on the fuel pump." An excellent remedy. The cold liquid pulls the fuel into the pump valves, which don't pump air, only liquid. Common on late model non-fuel-injected cars in the hot summer. One more reason why fuel injection has been substituted on many cars.

variable intake control — on new Yamaha-engined V-6s (Taurus S40, Toyota MR2, etc.), with two sets of tuned intake pipes, the engine runs up to 3800 rpm on 12 valves, but above 3800 rpm, 24 valves. A "kitten-monster" engine in one.

vatche carros — street urchins in Mexican border towns like Juarez who would run up to your car and say "vatche carro?". It was wise to employ them, as they would watch your car in any case, and if not paid their pittance (it was cheap anyways!) would collect in lieu of payment anything they could extract from the car, by any means. If, however, they were holding up a wet rag, it meant "wash your car?" and as the rag usually had gravel in it, you'd probably lose more in scratches than you would by theft.

ventilated crankcase — overheard wrecking yard owner Paul Frels on the phone to a cohort: "That's right, Mazda 626, looks great...it's got a ventilated crankcase, only $500." A connecting rod has let go and is sticking out through the block....i. e. needs a motor. See also **flower pot engine, planter.**

Venturi — carburetor throat or barrel. Four-barrel carbs are sometimes known as "4 V"s. The Venturi principle is a restriction in size in the throat of the carburetor which causes pressure drop, which in turn causes fuel to be drawn into flow stream of carburetor and thus into engine. Ford once sold a "variable Venturi" carburetor.

Vespa — sexy Italian motorscooter. Civilized transport. Has a spare tire. "My first love."—Jim. "The engine—two stroke—actually *purrs*!" "Fantastic packaging, lousy weight distribution, instant wheelies."

Veteran — pre"classic" automobiles, but after **vintage.** I. e. Georgian (post World War I) cars up to, say, the 1931 Riley — "old as the industry, modern as the hour." —from Don Hackett. Anon. Brit.: up to 1905, Veteran. Before 1930, Vintage. The odd Bentley, Alvin etc. 1930-1940, p.v.t. s—post vintage thoroughbreds.

Vette — Corvette.
vette-renarians — Corvette specialty repair shops.

Vintage — oldest of the old cars, Edwardian (pre World War I), c. 1888-through such great old models as the 1903 Wolseley.

virgin — spotless, unwrecked, rare and clean. "Yessir," Artie says, "this one's a virgin. Never been **kissed.**"

virgin fuel filter — see **slut fuel filter.**

Vista — 1959-60 Pontiac **"greenhouse" four-door hardtop convertible,** according to the Cool Car Club newsletter (Austin TX Sept.-Oct. 1988). See also **"steamboat-bridge" rear windows, Holiday.**

VW Scirocco — the hot rods of Europe. Hot cams and four valve per cylinder heads are available and relatively cheap. Light and fast.

W

wa - deeg or **wa-deej** — sound of impact....hence, the impact itself, the brute physical force ("he put the old wa-deeg to it!")

wake bumps — another name, according to writer Willie Mae Williams, for **drunk bumps.**

walking it — "to dominate a race from start to finish." —from C. H. B. in the San Antonio *Current* the day before the San Antonio Gran Prix (1988). This term comes from cards, especially games where "tricks" are "taken," and is used when a lowish card unexpectedly wins the trick: "and the deuce **walks!**"

walking man's special — used car salesman's term for a car that has dents, chugs a bit, but runs. See also **note lot (don't walk, see Hawk).**

walking short — nickname for a short fat, unfriendly, chip-on-shoulder traffic cop. As opposed to "walking tall," Buford Pusser, of movie fame.

warped — bent metal surface....such as that on yer cylinder head....caused by running out of coolant, etc. and getting very hot..... Don't, don't, don't "run in the red" (with the heat gauge "pegged", i. e. all the way over, pinned to the peg.)

Wartburg — squat, rounded, small Eastern bloc automobile easily recognized by its refrigerator-like styling and the distinctive diamond in its grille. Built at the old VW plant, abandoned after the partitioning of Germany after World War II.

war wagon — Toyota 4-wheel drive vehicle, so identified because its owner (in Texas) had heard that in the Chad/Libya war these vehicles were used effectively against tanks when five or so guns were mounted on them.

waste gate — device, part of turbo system, which controls turbo boost by spilling excess force, pressurization. The pressure is "dumped", usually when a pre-set limit is reached.

water buffalo — nickname for 70s Suzuki, watercooled two-stroke triple cylinder motorcycle. Big, clumsy, powerful, ugly. Original paint scheme was purple and white!

water car — a used car, bought at auction, often sold as a "good car," which turns out upon inspection to have high-water marks on e. g. the sunvisors, and trouble with electrical systems and instruments, never works right.

water Porsche — a water-cooled Porsche (models 944, 928, 924), considered inferior to the air-cooled models used in racing.

wave start — way to start a motorcycle race in which two classes are to be run at the same time. They go out in two waves, and the second wave has to keep their hands up until the proper time is signaled for their start. See also **clutch start, Le Mans start, hand on helmet start.** —from Rod Root.

wedge — the Chrysler 426, from the shape of the combustion chamber. Among other, especially British car fans, this term refers to the Triumph TR-7, from its body shape.

in the **weeds** — two meanings: said of a policeman who hides behind, say, a roadside billboard, to dash out from concealment and catch speeders. But also, said of a low-slung car.

weenie roaster — jetpowered hot rod racing car.

weight watcher — trucker's term for otherwise **plain-jane** highway patrol car. This one usually has a little antenna, red lights *behind* grilles, and likes to catch overloaded trucks (for a big fine); it even weighs them with portable truck scales in the trunk of the plain-jane car. The small portable scales weigh one axle at a time.

welders — really good welders are bragged on by the mechanics they work for, on how fine their work is. "He could weld the legs back onto a flea." The real hard jobs are genuinely difficult. "Gee, Jim, you welded that shattered oil pan just like new" (the oil pan had been shattered by a curb at 30 plus mph.)

wets — racing tires for rain. See **slicks.**

wet sleeve — Renault/Volvo/deLorean engine. Let's just put it this way: you can't do just a valve job on one of these. By pulling the cylinder heads, you "disturb" the seal on the wet sleeves, which must be pulled—pistons, rods, bearings—off the crank, etc., in order to reseal the internals of the motor.

WFO — wide fucking out, i. e. opened up all the way, **balls to the wall.**

whale-tail — the Turbo Porsche, from the appearance of its ass-end, with its whale-tail-like turbo intake.

wheel-hop — what happens if you have a bad suspension and accelerate hard. To resist this tendency, see **traction bars, ladder bars.**

wheelie — to **burn off** so skillfully that the front wheel comes off the ground. Usually done with motorcycles, but it can be done with a car, too. **Wheelie** is short for "wheelstand". Compare **stoppie.** (Brit.)

wheelie bars — on drag racers, chrome bars that stick out of the back of the car to limit the front end lift effect as the car **peels out**, actually to *prevent* the wheelie, to force more of the torque into forward propulsion.

wheel man — gangster term for driver of getaway car.

wheelspin — burning off. Overabundance of force placed on the driving wheels, causing them to spin under acceleration.

it can feel the **whipass** coming — said of the extraordinary compliance with your wishes which a piece of machinery shows when you get out the impact wrench.

whiskered plug — spark plug with tiny piece of carbon or metal bridging the gap, thus eliminating the spark and making that cylinder miss out. Can be caused by overheating, water getting into the cylinder, lead in fuel in a 2-stroke,or excessive wear. See also **arced plug.**

whiskey bump, whiskey dent — a small, or not so small, bit of damage to a fender, etc.

white belt, white shoes, fat, friendly — essentials of a used car salesman.

Whitworth wrench sizes — old obsolete English system of sizing nuts according to the stud they screw onto rather than the head of the nut. Probably the reason why English cars have more **chingered**

nuts and bolts than any other kind of car.

whompy jawed — archaic but still used to mean "hit and hit hard, out of alignment, bent" as in a bent bumper or frame.

whoops — or "whoop-de-doos". A series of little or not so little humps in a dirt race track. Also known as a "thank-you-ma'am" (from "Wham, Bam, Thank-you, Ma'am").

whop stick — a hammer. Also known as the **inertia wrench.** See also **fine tuner, Harley tuning wrench.**

why learn the English system of measurement?! — i. e. feet, inches, etc. "Who cares what the distance from the King of England's tip of his nose to his fingertip is?" —Ralf Schmidt, BMW mechanic.

Wide Track — Pontiac's name for the 1959 Bonneville Vista, which was in fact so wide that Patrick Bedard, in the January 1989 *Car and Driver,* called it "the Vista's USS *Forrestal* body," a reference to a famous aircraft carrier. Pontiac continued to use the term "wide track" for many years.

widowmaker — a fearsomely rugged, steep hill, in racing events such as hillclimbs, for both cars and motorcycles. One such, near Helotes, Texas, has a treeline at top of crag that prevents anyone gaining safety of the crest. Widowmakers are *steep* mothers, and when you lose it, as 90% of entrants do, you bail off the bike to the side, not below. A particularly bad curve on a road race may also be known as a widowmaker. As also the Yamaha RZ 350, all Ninjas, etc. and the F-104.

windscreen — British term for "windshield."

wing ding — derisive name for small two-stroke motorcycles. See also **bing bing.** From the sound they make, like an angry amplified mosquito.

wing (rear) — "actually an upside-down airfoil on the back of the car which provides aerodynamic downforce." —from CHB. The Chaparral racing car had a front wing, too, which was so damned effective it had to be declared illegal.

wings, mudguards — British terms for fenders.

winkers — turn signals. (Brit.) Also **flashers.**

winnie wasto — Winnebago.

winning ugly — winning the race, but pissing everyone else off with your aggressive driving, bragging, etc.

and **wipe the blood off too!** — remark, tossed to fledgling mechanic, along with the keys to the sports car he was about to fix....(a difficult job, a **knucklebuster**, for a bitchy, uptight customer who probably won't appreciate one's efforts anyway). A two-fold warning to the mechanic.

W-motor — the 348-349 Chevrolet engine, 1958-64, from the shape of the valve cover.

wooden steering wheels — pretty, even beautiful but did you ever see one of these splintered after a crash.....ooohh....think it over and always buckle up your belt.

woodie — a station wagon with wood trim, a much-prized vehicle in the 1950s in North America.

worm — racing sidecar rig — low, prone driver, wide slick rear tire. (Brit.)

wowo — Volvo.

wrench — American term for **spanner.**

wrenching — lowbrow mechanicing, performing basic mechanic labor.

"Wurlitzer" dashboard — 50s Plymouths and Dodges had lots of chrome, symmetry, accent on the center of the dash, where the radio provided music.

Y

yammer-hammer — A Yamaha. —Leonard Zwilling, staff, *Dictionary of American Regional English.*

yard dogs — cars you buy at auction, thinking they'll sell quick, but which don't sell. —Artie Osborn, Red River Motors, Austin. The term is itself a joke, for in Texas, a "yard dog" is a dog you bought as a hunting dog, but all he does is eat and sleep, and when you want to go hunting, "he crawls under the pickup."

Yank tank — Canadian Maritimers' term, also British, for any big American car.

yell and hit it — what some Dads always did when the car broke down, not knowing any other procedure: "he would just yell and hit it!"

yellow bumper — "Freshman driver in NASCAR competition. During his first season, ...a driver is required to have a yellow rear bumper on his car to let other drivers know that he's a novice. As a result, the newcomer himself is called a yellow bumper." —from John Lawlor, *How to talk car*.

yielding to tonnage — no law specifically outlines this....but self preservation dictates that dump trucks that want to run stop signs, etc., get their path opened (or else).

yogurt makers — jocular term for any French car—Peugeot, Renault, Citroen. See also **frog car.**

Z

Zagato — Italian bodymaker. Designer of the Ferrari, Alfa, Aston Martin, etc.

Z car — the Datsun Z-series (240, 260, 280, 300 ZX series). A **Jap Jag.**

zebra crossing — British term for a marked pedestrian crossing (because it has diagonal stripes).

Zebra-stripe upholstery — "I got it," Ace brags, "because of that joke where the zebra escapes from the zoo and upon wandering into a horse farm and being confronted by the stud, "What are you?" he asks. "I'm a Zebra," she says. "What are you?" "I'm the stud hereabouts." "And what do you do?" she asks. "Take off those pajamas you have on and I'll show you."

Zen driving — "In Zen driving, you simply accept a traffic jam and become one with it." "If somebody cuts you off, you simply acknowledge your anger and then let it go." —Kevin and Todd Berger, *Zen Driving* (1988).

to **zip it up** — to finish a job. Probably adapted from surgery.
zip strips — see **rumble strips.**

Zuffenhausen — where Porsches are designed? (They're made in Stuttgart). On Porsche posters: "Rennwagen from Zuffenhausen."

Acknowledgements

Thanks for help to Freeland Reynolds Jr. (Nova Scotia's South Shore), Grant Curtis, Tim McCrary (formerly of Carosserie Roxboro), Hugh and David Jones (NS South Shore, Rossignol Motors), Aaron Poteet, Dewey Poteet, Chris Coyle, Jonathan Sommer, Erwin Schieder (body man, Bromont Québec), Tony Bell, Artie Osborn, (Austin's Washington Motors — "won't lie to ya"), Greg Hirsch and the gang at International Car Parts, Austin, Rod Root (American Motor Cycle Association expert cardholder, on the Triumph 750 twin), and Charles H. Booker (writer for the San Antonio *Current),* and Paul Burrill, Madison WI. Thanks also to Don Hackett for many entries and especially for his shared airplane talk, Tom Brown, John Lepine, Diane Rothberg, Victor Janoff, and others too numerous to mention. Some entries from Texas car talk also appear in Ken Weaver's *Texas Crude* (New York: 1984); others are quoted from Robert Appel's *The Used Car Believer's Handbook* (Toronto: Dorset, 1979). John Lawlor's *How to talk car* (Chicago: Topaz Felsen Books, 1965), *the* guide to hot rod terms, is sampled through half a dozen entries quoted here, but is unmatched as a guide to the drag racing and 50s modified car world, and it is illustrated with great black-and-white old photos of funny cars and rail jobs, etc. Mike Fox and Steve Smith's *Rolls-Royce: The Complete Works (The best 599 Stories about the World's Best Car (* London: Faber and Faber, 1984) is similarly quoted in half-a-dozen entries, and contains many fine stories about this fine, expensive automobile.

Special thanks toJohn Mahoney of Pigwideon Press, for editorial services, and to Jim Bell and Judith Larue of Austin's Alphagraphics, Richard Bradford and the staff of Loyola computer centre, Concordia University, Montreal, and Martin Stone and Susan Kazenel.